Chiweenies.

The Ultimate Chiweenie Dog Manual

Chiweenie care, costs, feeding, grooming, health and training all included.

by

George Hoppendale

and

Asia Moore

The Ultimate Chiweenie Dog Manual
Copyrighted © 2014
Author: George Hoppendale
Author: Asia Moore - Ask a Dog Whisperer
K-9SuperHeroesDogWhispering.com

Published by: IMB Publishing

Table of Contents

Table of Contents

About the Authors

George Hoppendale is an experienced writer and a true animal lover. He enjoys writing animal books and advising others how to take care of their animals to give them a happy home.

Asia Moore is an animal lover, professional Dog Whisperer, Cynologist and Author, living on Vancouver Island, off the west coast of British Columbia, in Canada, who believes that all humans and dogs can live together in harmony.

She and her dog whispering team, which includes an 8-year-old Shih Tzu named Boris, teach dog psychology to humans, to help alleviate problem behaviors that arise through misunderstandings between humans and their canine counterparts so that everyone can live a happy and stress-free life together.

Visit Asia and her dog whispering team online at:
K-9SuperHeroesDogWhispering.com

Chapter 1: Introduction

The Ultimate Chiweenie Dog Manual will answer all the questions you may have when considering sharing your home with this cute and cuddly intelligent mixed breed.

Learn everything there is to know, including little known facts and secrets, and how to care for every aspect of the Chiweenie's life.

This Manual contains all the information you need, from birth to the Rainbow Bridge, including transitioning through house breaking, care, feeding, training and end of life, so that you can make a well-informed decision about whether or not the Chiweenie is the breed for you.

As well, this manual contains a great deal of information, tips and tricks that can easily be applied to any breed of dog.

Chapter 2: The Chiweenie Hybrid

The "Chiweenie" or *"Chiwee"* is a cross between a Chihuahua and a Dachshund, where one parent is a purebred Chihuahua and the other parent is a purebred Dachshund.

When two purebred canines are bred together, in the past they were simply referred to as *"mutts"*. Now, when two separate breeds are intentionally crossed or mixed together, they are often referred to as *"designer"* or *"hybrid"* dogs.

The most obvious mark of a *"designer"* or *"hybrid"* dog' is that the resulting puppies are named with what is referred to as a *"portmanteau"* word, which is a word that is a combination of two or more words, syllables or sounds that have been taken from the names of the two or more purebred parents, that becomes the new name of the designer breed.

The term *"designer dog"* has been traced back to the late 20th century, when breeders first began to cross purebred Poodles with other purebred canines with the intent of creating offspring that would retain the Poodle hypoallergenic coat, as well as traits considered desirable from other popular breeds.

Therefore, in order to better understand this hybrid dog, we need to first consider the traits of both breeds separately.

Although cross breed dogs are not recognized by purebred registries, such as the American Kennel Club (AKC), they are recognized by the International Designer Canine Registry (ICDR), where the Chiweenie designer dog is generally considered to be a small breed.

When purchasing a hybrid or designer breed canine, you need to keep in mind that while purebred dogs have been carefully bred for many generations to be recognizable by their consistently uniform look, size and temperament, puppies that are produced from combining one breed with another, such as in the case of the Chihuahua and Dachshund, may not inherit the same consistent traits from the breeding parents.

This means that puppies born in the same litter can have an appearance that is remarkably different from each of their other siblings, and it can also mean that each litter produced by this type of pairing may be unique.

While the appearance and size of a Chiweenie will largely depend upon the appearance and size of both parents, however, many of them seem to take on more of the traits of the Dachshund with the lighter coloring of the Chihuahua and shorter legs.

The type of coat may be more typically smooth, like the Chihuahua and Dachshund both have, or if the Dachshund parent is a longer or curlier haired Dachshund, the resulting Chiweenie puppies may have longer or curlier coats, or the litter of puppies may each land somewhere in between the two purebred parents, producing a coat with a slight wave or curl.

A Chiweenie can take on the physical appearance of the Dachshund, with the long low body and floppy ears, or the more square appearance of the Chihuahua, with longer legs and the erect ears typical of the Chihuahua breed.

When measured at the shoulder, the Chiweenie will usually stand no taller than 8 inches (20.3 cm) and weigh 10 pounds or less (4 kilograms) depending on the size of both parents.

No matter which side of the parenting combination the puppies take after, the Chiweenie will usually be a high energy small dog who will love to run and play.

1. Chihuahua

The Chihuahua, smallest of the "toy" breeds, takes its name from the state of Chihuahua in Mexico.

This breed has a very long history with an identical likeness of the Chihuahua being discovered in a wheeled dog toy found in Veracruz, Mexico, dating back as far as 100 AD. There is significant evidence to indicate that the Chihuahua breed was in Mexico at least 1400 years before the arrival of the first Europeans.

A rather disturbing piece of information discovered in a letter written in 1520 by Hernan Cortes, who was the Spanish Conquistador who led an expedition that caused the fall of the Aztec empire, indicated that the Aztecs raised and sold these small dogs as a food source.

Throughout the Chihuahua's very long history, this feisty, tiny breed of dog has maintained its popularity.

The American Kennel Club and the United Kennel Club both recognize the long and short-coated Chihuahua as a purebred canine, with the Chihuahua entering the official ranks of the American Kennel Club in 1904.

The Chihuahua, nicknamed the *"Chi" or "Chi-Chi"*, although very good at hunting bugs and small vermin for food have never been large enough to serve humans, other than for companionship or to bark a warning when strangers approach.

The Chihuahua has also been known as the *"Arizona dog"* or the *"Texas dog"* because of their close proximity to Mexico, which also helped to bring the Chihuahua into popularity throughout North America.

As what has happened to many smaller dog breeds over the years, original Chihuahua was thought to be a larger dog that was selectively bred for a smaller size.

Some believe that the original Chihuahua descended from the Techichi, which was a small dog living in central and northern Mexico between 900 and 1200 AD.

The coat of the Chihuahua does shed and is either short and straight, or longer and curly. The coat of a long haired Chihuahua may take up to three years to fully develop, usually is softer and sheds less than the smooth-coated dog and does not require clipping.

While common coat colors are black, brown, chocolate, cream, fawn, red, or mixed black and white, a Chihuahua coat can be solid colored or any variety or pattern of color.

The Chihuahua is an intelligent, easy to train dog with a large personality, that can be high energy in a small package.

They enjoy activity and can excel in canine sports such as Agility and Obedience because what they love the most is being with their humans.

When combined with their naturally active nature, this feisty companion may require plenty of physical and mental stimulation, involving long walks as well as games and training so that they do not become bored and develop unwanted behaviors.

The Chihuahua has a reputation for being snappish with younger children and other dogs, and they can be easily provoked to attack, especially if their human guardians do not properly socialize and train them.

The Chihuahua generally tends to prefer the company of other Chihuahuas or smaller dogs, which is also a natural way for them to protect themselves when in the company of much larger dogs who could inadvertently harm them during play.

If this feisty little dog is permitted to rule the roost, they will take on this role with a passion and will not hesitate to attack any person or other animal that may comes into close proximity to their beloved guardian. This type of problem is often further exacerbated when the guardian carries around their Chihuahua, giving them an even higher position of authority and control over their world.

This tiny dog takes its companionship role seriously, is most happy when with their guardian 24/7, and if not given a firm guiding hand will easily become jealous of other humans and pets.

As the Chihuahua breed does not display the submissive temperament seen in many other small lap dogs, they are not typically recommended as a good choice for homes with young children as a Chi can become snappy and overprotective.

This is a tiny dog that will not hesitate to use its teeth if it feels it must protect itself from rough or inappropriate handling.

In America, the Chihuahua was amongst the top ten dogs rated for popularity, reaching the #9 position in 2002, likely because of the very popular Gidget, who was featured as a talking Chihuahua in a Taco Bell advertising campaign.

Statistics indicate that the Chihuahua continues to rank highly in popularity, having remained amongst the top 13 most registered breeds for the past 10 years.

While the American Kennel Club weight standard for the Chihuahua breed states that for show purposes the dog must not weigh more than 6 pounds (2.7 kilograms), many Chihuahuas are considerably larger.

In the UK, for showing purposes, the British standard prefers a weight of between 4 and 6 pounds (1.8 and 2.7 kilograms).

The Chihuahua is not a good choice for a family with young children.

2. Dachshund

The feisty and active Dachshund is often referred to as a *"wiener"* dog because they are low to the ground with short legs and a long body.

This strong willed purebred, belonging to the hound category of canines, which originated in Germany, will live an average lifespan of 12 to 14 years.

Originally the standard sized Dachshund was bred to scent, chase and flush badgers and other animals living in burrows, while the smaller, miniaturized version was bred for hunting rabbits, squirrels or prairie dogs.

The name given to this fearless, energetic, yet stubborn hound breed, in German, literally means *"Badger Dog"*.

While the common coat color of a Dachshund is red or black with tan points, they can also be seen in a wide variety of color variations and patterns including dappled.

As a result of their long, low to the ground body shape, they are also often nicknamed the *"Sausage"* dog.

The Dachshund is bred in three distinctly different sizes, most commonly including Standard and Miniature and the less recognized Kaninchen (German for rabbit).

Thus the Dachshund can weigh anywhere from 8 to 16 pounds (3.6 to 7.3 kilograms) and can have a smooth, long or wire-haired coat.

The Dachshund temperament, while usually playful, because of their hunting background, can be stubborn and more difficult to train. They will love to chase after birds, small animals or a favorite ball with great ferocity.

The Dachshund is very lovable and dedicated to their family, and with their keen sense of hearing, they can be great watchdogs that will always loudly alert you to anyone approaching.

This breed is not usually overly fond of strangers or other unknown dogs and can be known to show aggression if not well socialized.

This breed may also become noisy and destructive if left at home alone and if left outside on his or her own may easily escape the yard through a small space in the fencing, or dig their way to freedom.

The strong willed Dachshund is not a good choice for a first time dog owner, as they require a strong hand that will provide consistent training, rules and boundaries and a safe outlet for relieving pent up energy.

While the exact origin of the Dachshund, as with many other breeds, is not clearly known, the roots of this noble hound may go back as far as ancient Egypt.

Today's more modern Dachshund is a combination of German, English and French terriers and hounds. These dogs have enjoyed opulent surroundings in many courts across Europe, having also been favored by Queen Victoria.

Popularity of this breed amongst apartment dwellers keeps this purebred canine consistently amongst the top ten most popular breeds in the US.

3. History/Origin of the Chiweenie

Determining true origin of a specific breed of canine is always met with a certain degree of controversy and many different theories about the true origin of a breed.

In the case of the Chiweenie, which is the result of breeding a Chihuahua with a Dachshund, the resulting tiny puppies are impossible to resist, and likely have been around since the 1990's.

While the Chiweenie will usually be a loving, affectionate and sweet natured dog inside the home, that will follow you everywhere, depending on the particular dog, the hunting heritage of the Dachshund may take over when they get outside and see birds, rabbits or rodents to chase.

There is no doubt that the melding of the Chihuahua with the genes of the Dachshund has produced an energetic, small lap dog that will need plenty of daily exercise.

As with any hybrid canine, while they can take on the best traits of both breeds, they can also take on some of the less appealing traits of both breeds.

4. Chiweenie Secrets

The name *"Chiweenie"* is a meshing together of the first few letters of the Chihuahua with the nickname of the Dachshund (wiener dog) to make up this hybrid dog name.

This hybrid or *"designer dog"* breed is also sometimes referred to as a *"the Mexican Hotdog"* or *"German Taco"*.

While the crossbred canine pairing of the Chihuahua with the Dachshund is a fairly new hybrid canine, they were apparently bred in North America for the first time in the 1990's.

Please understand that much of the content written in this book can be applied to EVERY dog, because when it comes right down to it, a dog is a dog no matter what size, shape, colour, price tag or fancy breed name we humans might attribute to them.

Every dog has a uniquely wonderful set of gifts to share with their human counterparts, if only us humans would listen.

They "tell" us when they are unhappy, when they are bored, when they are under-exercised, yet often we do not pay attention, or we just think they are being badly behaved.

Many humans today are deciding to have dogs, instead of children, and then attempting to manipulate their dogs into being small (or large) fur children. This is having a seriously detrimental effect upon the health and behaviour of our canine companions.

In order to be the best guardians for our dogs, we humans need to have a better understanding of what our dogs need from us, rather than what we need from them, so that they can live in safety and harmony within our human environment.

Sadly, many of us humans are not well equipped to give our dogs what they really need and that is why there are so many homeless, abandoned and frustrated dogs.

As a professional dog whisperer who is challenged with the task of finding amicable solutions for canine/human relationships that have gone bad, once the humans understand what needs to be changed, almost every stressful canine/human relationship can be turned into a happy, forever after.

The sad part is that many humans are simply not willing to do the work and devote the time necessary to ensuring that their dog's needs are met.

Almost all canine problems are a direct result of ignorance or unwillingness on the part of the canine guardian to learn what the dog truly needs. Forget about the breed for the moment, because what the dog needs to be a happy and well-balanced family member has nothing to do with size, shape, colour or breed.

First and foremost, our dogs need to be respected for their unique canine qualities.

For millennia, dog has been considered *"Man's best friend"*, and in today's society, when we want to do the best by our canine companions and create a harmonious relationship, we humans need to spend more time receiving the proper training to learn how Man can be dog's best friend.

A Chiweenie is a dog and therefore can be "Man's best friend" providing that the human guardian gains the knowledge they need in order to create a happy environment for the dog.

That's the secret: if the human treats the dog well and understands what the dog needs, the dog will be happy and the owner will be happy. This applies to any dog, whether a Chiweenie or any other breed.

For example, it is not possible to write a book specifically about *"How to train a Chiweenie"* or specifically about what "The first few days with your Chiweenie" will entail, etc., as while basic training techniques apply for every small dog, every dog and every human/dog relationship will be unique.

For this reason, when referring to daily feeding, care, house training, training, socializing, etc., these chapters are not written to apply specifically to the Chiweenie breed, as this information can be applied equally successfully to any small dog.

It is absolutely true that *"With the proper training, Man can learn to be dog's best friend."*

Chapter 3: Breeding

1. Locating a Reputable Breeder

NOTE: this chapter is not about how to breed the Chiweenie, rather it is all about how to care for the dog.

Although a good breeder cannot guarantee the lifelong health of any puppy, they should easily be able to provide a prospective Chiweenie guardian with plenty of information about the health of the puppy's parents.

Prospective guardians should definitely ask the breeder what sort of health tests have been carried out on the parents of a puppy they may be considering purchasing.

For instance, a reputable breeder will have had their breeding dogs tested for hip, thyroid and eye problems and prospective puppy purchasers should always inquire about possible congenital problems the parents or grandparents of the puppy might have, including any premature deaths.

2. Meet the Parents

Meeting the mother and father of your new Chiweenie puppy can tell you a great deal about what the temperament and demeanor of your puppy will likely be when they grow into adulthood.

A Chiweenie puppy's personality or temperament will be a combination of what they experience in the early days of their environment when they are in the breeder's care, and the genes inherited from both parents.

Visiting the breeder several times, observing the parents, interacting with the puppies and asking plenty of questions will help you to get a true feeling for the sincerity of the breeder.

The early environment provided by the breeder and the parents of the puppies can have a formative impact on how well your puppy will ultimately behave as an adult dog.

3. Questions to Ask a Breeder

Get to know your breeder by asking them why they decided to breed the Chiweenie and how long they have been breeding.

Ask if the breeder will permit you to visit their facility and will they give you a tour?

Ask the breeder if they own both breeding parents, or if they do not, ask if they familiar with, or have worked closely with both parents of the Chiweenie puppy you may be considering.

Ask how often the breeder allows the females and males to breed and reproduce.

Ask if the breeder will allow you to see the other dogs in the kennel and notice whether the kennel is clean, well maintained and animal friendly.

Will the breeder permit you to see other adult dogs, or other puppies that the breeder owns, socialize together?

Pay attention to whether the breeder limits the amount of time that you are permitted to handle the Chiweenie puppies. A reputable breeder will be concerned for the safety and health of all their puppies and will only permit serious buyers to handle the puppies.

Check to find out if the breeder is registered or recognized by your local, state or national breed organization.

a) Medical Questions

Every reputable breeder will certainly ensure that their Chiweenie puppies have received vaccinations and de-worming specific to the age of the puppies.

Always ask the breeder what shots the puppy has received and when it was last de-wormed and ask for the name of the breeder's veterinarian.

If you discover that the breeder has not carried out any of these procedures or they are unable to tell you when the last shots or de-worming was carried out, look elsewhere.

Also ask to see the breeder's veterinarian report on the health of the puppy you may be interested in purchasing, and if they cannot produce this report, look elsewhere.

b) Temperament Questions

You will want to choose a puppy with a friendly, easy going and congenial temperament and your breeder should be able to help you with your selection.

A good breeder will have noticed personality and temperament traits very early on in their Chiweenie puppies and should be able to provide a prospective purchaser with valuable insight concerning each puppy's unique personality.

Also ask the breeder about the temperament and personalities of the puppy's parents and ask what they have done to socialize the puppies.

Ask how old the puppies must be before they can be taken to their new homes. If the breeder is willing to let their puppies go any earlier than 10 weeks of age, they are more interested in making a profit than in the health of their puppies.

Always be certain to ask if a Chiweenie puppy you are interested in has displayed any signs of aggression or fear, because if this is happening at such an early age, you may experience behavioral troubles when the puppy becomes older.

c) Guarantee Questions

A reputable Chiweenie breeder will be interested in the lifelong health and wellbeing of all of their puppies and good breeders will want you to call them should a problem arise at any time during the life of your Chiweenie puppy.

As well, a good breeder will want you to return a puppy or dog to them, if for some reason you are unable to continue to care for it, rather than seeing the dog go to a shelter or rescue facility.

If the Chiweenie breeder you are considering does not offer this type of return policy, find one who does, because no ethical breeder would ever permit a puppy from one of his or her litters to end up in a shelter.

d) Return Contract

Reputable breeders offer return contracts. They do this to protect their reputation and to also make sure that a puppy they have sold that might display a genetic defect will not have the opportunity to breed and continue to spread the defect, which could weaken the entire breed.

Breeders also offer return contracts because purchasing a hybrid Chiweenie puppy from a breeder can be an expensive proposition, and if you find out that the puppy has a worrisome genetic defect, this could cost you a great deal with respect to unexpected veterinarian care. In such cases, most good breeders offer a return policy, and will be happy to give you another puppy.

e) Testimonials

Ask a Chiweenie breeder you are considering to provide you with testimonials from some of their previous clients, and then actually contact those people to ask them about their experience with the breeder, and the health and temperament of their Chiweenie dog.

A good breeder has nothing to hide and will be more than happy to provide you with testimonials because their best recommendation is a happy customer.

f) Breeder Reputation

The Internet can be a valuable resource when researching the reputation of a Chiweenie breeder. For instance, you will be able to post on most forums discussing breeders to quickly find out what you need to know from those who have first hand experience.

Also, be prepared to answer questions the breeder may have for you, because a reputable breeder will want to ask a prospective purchaser their own questions, so that they can satisfy themselves that you are going to be a good caretaker for their puppy.

First, do your homework about the Chiweenie breed and then carry out as much research as possible about the specific breeder you are considering before making your initial visit to their facility.

The more information you have gathered about the Chiweenie breed, and the breeder you are considering and the more information the breeder knows about you, the more successful the match will be.

Chapter 4: Vital Statistics

1. Countries of Origin

Mexico and Germany are the countries of origin for the Chihuahua and the Dachshund and as you might imagine, since these are both purebred canines that have been around for a very long time, there is no way to know for sure when or who decided to first intentionally put these two breeds together to create the hybrid Chiweenie.

2. Litter Size

On average, 2 to 6 puppies per litter.

3. Height and Weight

The Chiweenie is considered to be a smaller breed, and depending upon whether the Chihuahua is bred to a Toy or Miniature Dachshund, they will generally weigh between 4 and 14 pounds (1 and 6 kilograms) and stand between 6 and 9 inches (15.2 and 22.8 centimeters) when measured at the withers (top of the shoulder).

4. Temperature & Heart Rate

Temperature: 100.5 to 102.5 degrees Fahrenheit (38.05 to 39.16 Celsius).

Respiratory Rate: 10 to 20 per minute

Pulse: Puppies, 120 to 160 per minute. Adults, 60 to 140 per minute.

Gums: should be pink

5. Lifespan

On average, the Chiweenie lifespan will be between 12 and 15 years, with some living even longer.

6. Intelligence

Stanley Coren, a professor of psychology at the University of British Columbia, in Vancouver, B.C., Canada, published *The Intelligence of Dogs* in 1994. Since then this book has become the standard for rating the particular intelligence of different canine breeds.

Coren's book describes three categories of dog intelligence:

(1) *instinctive intelligence*;

(2) *adaptive intelligence*, and

(3) *working and obedience intelligence*.

Instinctive intelligence refers to a dog's ability to carry out tasks it was bred to perform, such as guarding, herding, hunting, pointing, retrieving, or supplying companionship.

> *"Adaptive intelligence refers to how well a dog is able to solve problems on its own.*
>
> *Working and obedience intelligence refers to how quickly a dog is able to learn from humans."*

As the Chiweenie is a combination of two purebred canines, we need to look at the intelligence of each breed separately to get an idea of what the intelligence is likely going to be for the Chiweenie hybrid.

According to the findings of Stanley Coren, the Chihuahua breed ranks 27 out of a possible 79 in the *"Fair Working/Obedience Intelligence"* category.

In other words, if one is to agree with the findings of Stanley Coren, on the Chihuahua side of this hybrid, this dog can understand new commands after 40 to 80 repetitions and obey first commands approximately 30% of the time.

Further, Stanley Coren ranks the Dachshund #49 out of a possible 79 in the *"average working/obedience intelligence"* category, which means that the Dachshund can understand new commands after 25 to 40 repetitions and will obey first commands only 50% of the time, or better.

The outcome of the pairing of these two purebreds, depending upon which breed's genes are more dominant, could mean that the Chiweenie will take on the *"average"* intelligence of the Dachshund, or the *"fair"* intelligence of the Chihuahua, or may be somewhere between the two.

Please keep in mind that there are always exceptions to every study and a particular breed's degree of intelligence can often be related to their upbringing and how they are trained.

No matter which side of the parent lineage the intelligence of this canine follows, or whether they land somewhere in the middle, in the case of the Chiweenie, there is no doubt that this designer dog will be a happy, active and loving little companion.

7. Living Conditions

The Chiweenie, because of their smaller size, does not require an expansive living environment in order to be happy. This small breed will be perfectly fine living in an apartment or condominium complex.

However, this will be an energetic little dog, requiring both mental and physical stimulation that they will receive from daily exercise outside of the home.

A full grown Chiweenie will need to burn off their daily pent up energy by going for at least two good walks of 30 minutes to an hour each beside their human companions every day.

In order for this little dog to be happy and well balanced they will want to be close to their human family. This means taking your Chiweenie everywhere with you, which also helps to socialize and exercise their intelligent brains.

Leaving a loving and bright little dog home alone for many hours every day will be torture for them that could result in the Chiweenie becoming destructive and/or noisy.

8. Hybrid Vigor

Remember those stories you used to hear when you were a kid when people talked about dogs and how a *"mutt"* was the best kind?

What you may have heard about *"mutts"* being healthier and making better pets is not just an old wife's tail, because it can actually be quite true.

The term *"hybrid vigor"* (also called Heterosis) is a real phenomenon that occurs in every animal (& plant) species during the first pairing or crossing when two separate species are bred together.

Therefore, although all Chiweenie dogs will not be a first generation cross between a Chihuahua and a Toy or Miniature Dachshund, those who are will likely be healthier and mentally more stable than either of the litter's purebred parents.

When both parents share the same traits, in a purebred line, the offspring they produce will be much more likely to display a disease or health problem common to the breed.

On the other hand, while puppies resulting from breeding two distinctly different purebred canines will usually retain physical attributes common to both parents, the puppies will display characteristics which lie somewhere between the two parents.

With respect to health issues, if only one purebred parent carries a trait or health problem common to the breed, when breeding these two purebreds together, this gene will be recessive in the puppies.

With the birth of each successive generation of puppies, where a Chiweenie is bred to another Chiweenie, the hybrid vigor will be lost because the more inbreeding that occurs, the more genes the Chiweenie will share in common with the breed parents, which can result in them being prone to more health issues.

Of course, just because the Chiweenie is a crossbreed does not guarantee that the puppies produced will be a combination of the best of each of their parents because despite how conscientious a breeder may be, the way genetics will combine when two different breeds are put together cannot be exactly controlled.

Chapter 5: Temperament

No matter which side of the family a puppy takes after, a Chiweenie is most likely going to be an energetic dog who loves to run and play.

Because of their diminutive size, although every dog needs the discipline of being walked on leash outside of the home each day, they will not require a great deal of space and can be happy running around in the house or under supervision in a small, secure backyard.

These dogs bond strongly to humans of all ages, although they may prefer one family member over all others, and because of their smaller size, a Chiweenie needs to be protected from very young children or encounters with larger dogs.

Chiweenies are very alert and make excellent small watchdogs with a big bark. It takes a very stealthy stranger to sneak up on one of these little guys.

Remember that despite their small size, both of these breeds are fearless, and because the Dachshund side of the equation was originally a hound dog used for hunting badgers and other small prey, if not well trained and given the opportunity, they may take off after birds, rabbits, cats or other small animals.

While this breed will likely become very attached to its family members, they may not be particularly friendly toward strangers or other dogs unless continually socialized.

This is an affectionate, energetic, fun-loving, and active small breed that will enjoy plenty of exercising.

If you neglect this dog and do not provide them with regular daily exercise and mental stimulation, they will create their own entertainment, which could include destroying your property or barking to excess.

The Chiweenie will need to be well and continually socialized at a young age, and involved in all of the family's activities, otherwise they may become unhappy barkers.

Some Chiweenies may be social butterflies, while others may stick closely to their immediate family members.

1. Behavior With Children and Pets

Generally speaking, the smaller Chiweenie, because of their more independent, feisty and active natures may not be the best choice for families with young children or for older adults who may not be mobile enough to give them the exercise they need.

Both the Chihuahua and the Dachshund breeds prefer the company of their own kind and unless well socialized with other animals, the Chiweenie may bark, growl and display aggressive tendencies toward other dogs and pets.

2. Is This Dog an Escape Artist?

The Chiweenie should never be left alone or unsupervised outside, even in a securely fenced yard.

This is a fearless, curious and bold little explorer, who when bored may find a way to squeeze under fences or through cracks to go exploring the neighborhood on their own.

As well, if given the time, they could become a digger and escape the yard this way.

Further, depending on the size of the Chiweenie, if they are smaller, they could easily become prey for large birds, such as hawks, owls or eagles.

Of course, all dogs will have a much higher urge to roam before they are spayed or neutered, therefore, early spaying or neutering of a Chiweenie puppy will go a long way toward helping to curb any wanderlust tendencies that may be a result of raging hormones.

Chapter 6: Before You Buy

Pros & Cons

No matter what breed you may be pondering as a possible candidate for sharing your home and life, this decision should never be entered into lightly.

As with any breed, those who may be considering a Chiweenie need to carry out research and make sure they have all the facts straight before taking the plunge because there are always many important factors to keep in mind.

Chiweenies are loving, active small athletes who will enjoy any sort of advanced training or obedience competition, such as Agility or Rally.

While the Chihuahua has a fair intelligence, a properly bred Chiweenie that takes after the Dachshund side of their genes, will likely be fairly easy to train, while stubborn and smart enough to get their own way if not given consistent rules and boundaries.

When treated kindly and trained with positive reinforcement, the Chiweenie can learn quickly and will love the attention.

If you are often away from home, this breed is not a good choice for you because both sides of this hybrid pairing can be stubborn, loud barkers, who will tell the world how unhappy they are not to be with you.

They will suffer greatly from loneliness and separation anxiety, as both sides of their lineage makes them a loving companion that wants to always be with their guardian.

The Chiweenie temperament will usually be feisty, inquisitive, friendly and loyal to their guardians.

This is a small dog that will do well with families who have older children, or active seniors who prefer a smaller dog.

1. Pros of Chiweenie Ownership

The Chiweenie has many good qualities to consider, including:

- playful and loving;

- smaller size makes them easy to transport;

- they do well in apartments;

- they live a relatively long life;

- moderately easy to train;

- excellent watch dogs;

- they like to be with their guardians 24/7.

2. Cons of Chiweenie Ownership

No matter what breed you choose, there will always be some downsides to carefully consider, including:

- tiny Chiweenie puppies are so adorable, which unfortunately means that they are a popular small breed. Simply because they are so cute means that they will also be a favorite of irresponsible, greedy puppy mill breeders, because small and *"cute"* is a big seller that does not require a lot of space for breeding;

- this is an active dog requiring daily exercising to keep them both physically and mentally healthy;

- strong attachment to their guardians means that they will not do well if left alone for long periods of time;

- they may bark and be destructive when left alone;

- this small breed can easily be hurt or injured, if handled roughly;

- this small dog can easily be harmed by larger animals;

- depending on the size of the dog, it could be snatched up by large birds of prey;

- not a good choice for a family with young children;

- this is a mildly shedding dog;

- they can be stubborn and take over the home if their guardian does not provide rules and boundaries;

- they may not particularly enjoy the company of other dogs;

- they could be strong willed which does not make them a good choice for a first time dog owner.

-

Chapter 7: Choosing the Right Dog

1. Where to Purchase a US Puppy

When wondering where to start your search for purchasing a Chiweenie puppy in the United States, there are several clubs and registries that will be good starting points, including:

The American Canine Hybrid Club (ACHC) is a hybrid registry service established in 1969.

The National Hybrid Registry (NHR) is a registry service for dog's from which both parents are verified to be pure bred dogs and eligible to be registered in the National Kennel Club.

The International Designer Canine Registry® (IDCR) is the World's Premier Designer Dog Registry and is dedicated exclusively to providing certified registration and pedigree services for all designer breeds. The IDCR also provides a list of registered breeders.

Greenfield Puppies (Pennsylvania) *"has been finding loving homes for puppies for over a decade. Breeders on our site are located throughout Pennsylvania and surrounding states. We expect every breeder to comply with all state laws and follow strict guidelines that we have put in place. We do not condone any puppy mills and strive to bring you only the best, well-loved puppies. We expect all Dog Breeders to guarantee the health of their puppies in accordance with their state's laws and guidelines. If you are looking for puppies for sale in PA, look no further."*

California Designer Breeds Breeders bring puppies and guardians together across North America. *"We help you find the ideal puppy for your family. We do not allow just any breeder to post puppies on our site, but have a thorough, systematic process that screens the breeders and health checks every puppy before they come home to you.*

We believe we have one of the most stringent Breeding Standards in the industry and approve less than 15% of those that apply to our network! Once approved, we randomly visit our breeders to ensure they adhere to our policies and also follow up regarding the health of the puppies, with families who bring home a puppy from one of our breeders. "

2. Where to Purchase a UK Puppy

Designer Dogs - The Kennel Club is a registration and information service to help prospective owners find Kennel Club "assured breeders" of both purebreds and cross breeds.

Little Rascals (located in Lincolnshire) are *"open seven days a week from 9am until 6:30pm, three hundred and sixty five days a year. We are always happy to help and are only a phone call away should you need our assistance and advice.*

Here at Little Rascals we strive to maintain and improve our high standards on a day-to-day basis. We have an independent vet who is on call whenever we need them, they make at least weekly visits to health check, vaccinate and microchip all our puppies.

All of our puppies make fantastic family pets with kind, loving natures.

Little Rascals is a part of Swindell's Livestock, a family owned business established since 1965. Here at Little Rascals we are licensed, experienced dog breeders with 10 permanent staff members working closely to ensure our stud dogs and puppies receive the best care twenty four hours a day, every day. "

3. Average Prices for Puppies

There is a wide range of *"average"* pricing for any designer or hybrid Chiweenie, with some adoptions or rescues beginning around $300 (£179).

There does not seem to be an "average" breeder pricing for Chiweenie puppies as pricing ranges widely between $180. and $650. (£107. and £388.), depending on the particular breeder.

4. Avoiding Puppy Mills or Farms

As soon as a particular breed of dog becomes popular, they also become particularly susceptible to being bred by disreputable, high profit *"puppy mills"* or *"commercial breeding farms"*.

Puppy Mill breeding is especially prevalent with cute, smaller breeds, such as the Chiweenie.

This inhumane and cruel world of canine pregnancy for profit occurs all over the world, and if you are not very careful about where and how you purchase your Chiweenie puppy, you may unknowingly end up promoting this disreputable practice.

Not only do Puppy Mills seriously contribute to overpopulation, they produce diseases, and genetically flawed puppies that may suffer greatly with behavioral and/or health related problems that will cost their guardians greatly in terms grief and stress and unexpected financial burden associated with veterinarian and behavioral costs, while the puppy's life may be cut prematurely short.

These dogs suffer in ways most of us could never imagine. For instance, most of these poor breeding dogs have never walked on solid ground or felt grass as they are housed in cramped wire cages their entire short lives.

Females are bred continuously until they can no longer produce puppies at which time they are sold to laboratories for experiments, killed or dumped on the side of a road.

Although the puppy mill problem is certainly not exclusive to the United States, as it happens all over the world, the problem is so rampant in the US that several states are actually labeled as "Puppy Mill States". These include Missouri, Nebraska, Kansas, Iowa, Arkansas, Oklahoma and Pennsylvania.

It can be difficult to shut down these mill or mass-producing farming operations because, just like the drug trade, it is business on a large and lucrative scale.

Although Puppy Mill puppies are sold in a variety of different venues, pet stores are the main source for selling these unfortunate puppies, who are taken away from their mothers far too young (at 4 to 5 weeks of age) and sold to brokers, who pack them into crates to ship them off to pet stores. Many innocent puppies die during transportation.

Think seriously before buying a puppy from a pet store because almost all puppies found in pet stores (whether or not the employees working there are aware of it) are the result of inhumane puppy mill breeding. If you purchase one of these puppies, you are helping to enable and perpetuate this horribly cruel breeding practice.

Every time someone buys a puppy from a pet store, the store will order more from the Puppy Mill. As far as the pet store is concerned, the puppies are simply inventory, like bags of dog food, and when one item drops off of the inventory list, another is purchased to replace it.

Puppy Mill puppies are also sold at flea markets, on the side of the road, at the beach, through newspaper ads and through fancy websites and Internet classifieds.

The only way to put these shameful, commercial businesses out of business is by spreading the word and never buying a puppy from a pet store, or any other advertising medium, unless you have first thoroughly checked them out by visiting the facility in person.

Always be wary if you answer an advertisement for a low priced puppy for sale and the person selling offers to deliver the puppy to you, because this could easily be the first sign that you are about to be involved in an illegal Puppy Mill operation.

Educate yourself and spread the word to others about Puppy Mills, because this is the first step toward ensuring that yourself and everyone you know are never unknowingly involved in the suffering that is forced upon the breeding dogs and puppies trapped in a puppy mill or mass farming operation.

5. How to Choose the Right Puppy

Choosing the right puppy for your family and your lifestyle is more important than you might imagine.

Many people do not give serious enough thought to sharing their home with a new puppy before they actually bring one home.

For instance, many of us choose a puppy solely based on what it looks like, because the breed may currently be popular, or because their family had the same kind of dog when they were growing up.

a) Important Questions

In order to be fair to ourselves, our family and the puppy we choose to share our lives with, we humans need to take a serious look at our life, both as it is today and what we envision it being in the next ten to fifteen years, and then ask ourselves a few important, personal questions, and honestly answer them, before making the commitment to a puppy, including:

41

Do I have the time and patience necessary to devote to a puppy, which will grow into a dog who needs a great deal of attention, training and endless amounts of my devotion?

Do I lead a physically active, medium or low intensity life? For instance, am I out jogging the streets daily or climbing mountains or would I rather spend my leisure time on the couch?

Do I like to travel a lot? Perhaps a dog small enough to travel in the plane cabin with me is a consideration.

Am I a neat freak? A low or non-shedding breed such as the Chiweenie, would make more sense.

Do I have a young, growing family that takes up all my spare time? A dog needs a lot of time and attention.

Am I physically fit and healthy enough to be out there walking a dog two to three times a day, every day, rain or shine (and much more when it's just a puppy)?

Can I afford the food costs and the veterinarian expenses that are part of being a conscientious dog guardian?

Is the decision to bring a puppy into my life a family decision, or just for the children, who will quickly lose interest?

Have I researched the breed I'm interested in, and is it compatible with my lifestyle?

What is the number one reason why I want a dog in my life?

Once you ask yourself these important questions and honestly answer them, you will have a much better understanding of the type of puppy that would be best suited for you and your family, and whether or not, it should be a Chiweenie.

If you are too busy for a dog, or choose the wrong dog, you will inevitably end up with an unhappy dog, which will lead to behavioral issues, which then will lead to an unhappy family and extra expense to hire a professional to help you reverse unwanted behavioral problems. Please take the time to choose wisely.

If you have absolutely decided that the Chiweenie is the right dog for you, the following tips will help you to choose the right puppy from the litter.

b) Careful Puppy Selection

Although your breeder can often help you with selecting the right puppy for you and your family, you will likely be feeling especially drawn to one puppy over another.

Although there are other considerations, how you feel toward a particular puppy in a litter is also an important part of deciding which pup to bring home.

Beyond your feelings, considering other factors will help improve the odds of you having a positive guardianship experience with your new Chiweenie puppy.

For instance, being a little objective when evaluating each puppy in the litter will help you to make the right choice.

While some people become very emotional when choosing a puppy and will be attracted to those who display extremes in behavior because they want to *"save"* them, it is not a particularly good idea to choose a puppy that may be very shy or frightened in the hope that they may grow into a happy, well-behaved dog.

Some people will delve even further into their emotional desires or needs to *"save"* or *"rescue"* and will choose a particular puppy because it has obvious health or behavioral issues, and because they want to provide it with a chance that they believe the puppy might not otherwise have.

While it is certainly wonderful that we humans have the capacity to raise and care for puppies that may be afflicted with health or behavior problems, it's important that these types of decisions are not undertaken lightly as such challenges can lead you down a path that could be an emotional roller coaster of highs and lows that can cause problems for both canine and human alike.

While many minor behavioral problems can be modified with early training, it's important to be aware that the time and effort needed to do so will be difficult to predict and you should be aware that *"rescuing"* a dog that could grow up to have behavioral problems may require the services of a professional dog whisperer or psychologist.

c) Pick of the Litter

Generally speaking, when choosing a puppy out of a litter, look for one that is friendly and outgoing, rather than one who is overly aggressive or fearful.

Taking note of a puppy's social skills, when they are still with their litter mates, will help you to choose the right puppy to take home because puppies who demonstrate good social skills with their litter mates are much more likely to develop into easy going, happy adults who play well with other dogs.

In a social setting where all the puppies can be observed together, make the following observations:

- when the puppies are playing, notice which puppies are comfortable both on top and on the bottom when play fighting and wresting with their littermates, and which puppies seem to only like being on top. Puppies who don't mind being on the bottom or who appear to be fine with either position, will usually play well with other dogs when they become adults.

- if the puppies have toys to play with, observe which puppies try to keep the toys away from the other puppies and which puppies share. Those who want to hoard the toys and keep all other puppies away may be more aggressive with other dogs over food or treats, or in play where toys are involved as they become older.

- notice which puppies seem to like the company of the other pups and which ones seem to be loners. Puppies who like the company of their littermates are more likely to be interested in the company of other dogs as they mature than anti-social puppies.

- observe the reaction of puppies who get yelped at when they bite or roughhouse with another puppy too hard. Puppies who ease up when another puppy yelps or cries are more likely to respond appropriately when they play too roughly as adults.

Also, check to see if the puppy you are interested in is sociable with people, because if they will not come to you, or display fear to strangers, this may be a problem when they become adults.

Further, always check if the puppy you are interested in is relaxed about being handled, because if they are not, they may become difficult with adults and children during daily interactions, during grooming or visits to the veterinarian's office.

6. How to Check If a Puppy is Healthy

Of course you will want to check if a puppy you are considering taking home is not just emotionally healthy, but also physically healthy.

First, ask to see veterinarian reports from the breeder to satisfy yourself that the puppy is as healthy as possible, and then once you make your decision to share your life with a particular puppy, make an appointment with your own veterinarian for a complete examination.

Before you get to this stage, however, there are a few general signs of good health to be aware of when choosing a healthy puppy from a litter, including the following:

- **Breathing** -- a healthy puppy will breathe quietly, without coughing or sneezing, and there will be no crusting or discharge around their nostrils;

- **Body** -- they will look round and well fed, with an obvious layer of fat over their rib cage;

- **Coat** – a healthy puppy will have a soft coat with no dandruff, dullness, greasiness or bald spots;

- **Energy** -- a well rested puppy will be alert and energetic;

- **Hearing** -- a healthy puppy with good hearing should react if you clap your hands behind their head;

- **Genitals** -- a healthy puppy will not have any sort of discharge visible in or around their genital or anal regions;

- **Mobility** – a healthy puppy will walk and run normally without wobbling, limping or seeming to be weak, stiff or sore; and

- **Vision**: -- a healthy puppy will have bright, clear eyes without crust or discharge and they should notice if a ball is rolled past them within their field of vision.

7. One Chiweenie, or Two?

While getting two Chiweenie puppies at once will be twice the fun, it will also be twice the work which means that you will need to be doubly alert and patient, and perhaps also lose even more sleep than you bargained for during the potty training phase.

Every puppy needs your constant attention and guidance, therefore, before taking the plunge, ask yourself if you have the time and energy to provide constant attention and guidance for two little puppies that could be running in opposite directions?

Many humans decide to get two puppies because they want their puppy to have someone to play with. Be careful that one of the reasons for this decision is not based on the fact that the human making this decision might not be the ideal candidate for having one puppy, let alone two.

For instance, if the reason you are considering two puppies is so that the one puppy will not be alone all day while you are at work, stop right there, because leaving one, two or a dozen puppies alone all day while you are at work is a terrible decision.

If this is your situation, you should NOT be considering any puppy at this stage of your life, and especially not one as loving and connected to their guardians as a Chiweenie who will suffer severely by being left alone

Another consideration when thinking about whether or not to get two puppies is that often when they grow up, there may be continual sibling rivalry as each puppy vies for your attention.

It is entirely possible that when the puppies mature, they will no longer get along with each as well as they once did when they were young puppies.

Further, when you have two puppies growing up together, one will always be the more dominant personality that will take over the other, and this could mean that neither puppy will fully develop their individual personalities.

As well, when you have two puppies or dogs in your life, they generally tend to be less affectionate or interested in their human guardians as they have each other in their own pack of dogs to rely upon. This can mean that they will focus so much on each other that they will bond much less with you, which can make it more difficult to train or convince either that you are the actual leader of the pack.

Each puppy will require your individual attention when it comes time for training, and having two puppies in the picture can make it very difficult for them to concentrate or focus on the job at hand.

For instance, when you are teaching puppy #1 to "Sit" while puppy #2 is trying to bite the tail of puppy #1, your job is going to be much more challenging.

Bottom line, most professional trainers or psychologists will advise that if you want two puppies, not to get them at the exact same time, from the same litter, so that you have the opportunity to house train and teach basic commands to one puppy before you bring another one into the home.

8. Best Age to Purchase a Puppy

Generally speaking, no puppy, including a Chiweenie puppy, should be removed from their mother any earlier than 8 weeks of age and leaving them until they are **10 to 16 weeks of age is preferred** because this will give them the extra time to learn important life skills from the mother dog, including eating solid food and grooming.

As well, leaving a puppy amongst their littermates for a longer period of time will help to ensure that they learn socialization skills.

Removing a puppy from the mother and other siblings too early could mean that they will miss out on valuable skills, and may not socialize well with others.

For the first month of a puppy's life they will be on a mother's milk only diet. Once the puppy's teeth begin to appear, they will start to be weaned from mother's milk and by the age of 8 weeks should be completely weaned and eating just puppy food.

Removing a puppy from their mother any earlier than eight weeks could mean they are not fully weaned and they would be much more difficult to feed.

9. Should I Get a Male or Female?

Everyone you ask will have a personal opinion about whether you should get a male or a female of any breed.

While you will find just as many humans preferring a male Chiweenie over a female Chiweenie, if you are a first time dog guardian, there may be a few considerations that can help you to make a more informed decision.

For instance, male dogs tend to want to mark or pee on anything upright (trees, telephone poles, tall grass, a stranger's leg) wherever they are out walking much more than females, however, a dominant female will also pee on three legs in an attempt to mark territory.

A male Chiweenie, even a housebroken one, may try to lift their leg on furniture when visiting a home where there are other dogs present.

When spaying and neutering your Chiweenie, the operation is much more invasive when spaying a female than the neutering process required for males.

Some humans pick their dogs based on sex alone because they cannot stop themselves from attributing human characteristics to their chosen dogs, and therefore believe that, for instance, a female dog will have a *"sweeter"* temperament, or a male dog may be more *"independent"*.

Of course, this is complete nonsense, because a dog is a dog, and it can be harmful to your relationship to project human emotions onto them or imagine that they will act like humans just because we are human.

Therefore, the best way to choose your Chiweenie puppy will be to take your time observing the litter when you visit the breeder.

10. The Chiweenie Shopping List

Before bringing home your new Chiweenie for the first time, there will be a list of items you need to make sure you have on hand, including:

- Food -- usually the puppy will remain on whatever food they have been fed at the breeder's for at least the first couple of weeks, until they are well settled in their new home, so make sure you ask the breeder what brand to buy;

- Food and Water Bowls -- make sure they are small enough for a young Chiweenie puppy to get into so that they can easily eat and drink.

- Kennel -- when you buy your puppy's hard-sided kennel, make sure that you buy the size that will be appropriate for them when they are full grown. It must be large enough so that (when full grown) they can easily stand up and turn around inside it;

- Martingale Collar, 2 Leashes and Harness -- buy the harness and collar small enough to fit your puppy and buy new collars as they grow larger.

- You will be able to keep the same leashes as all you will ever need is a four foot (1.22 meters) leash made out of nylon webbing with a light weight clip at the end (do not buy a leash that has a heavy clip on the end as it will be difficult for your puppy to carry around;

- Soft Beds (one or two) -- for them to sleep in when they are not in their kennel. Buy the beds large enough for a full grown Chiweenie;

- *"Sherpa"* or other type of soft-sided travel bag -- to get them used to traveling inside a carrier bag. Purchase the bag large enough to fit them when they are full grown and take it with you when you pick up your puppy from the breeder;

- Canine Shampoo and Conditioner;

- Finger Tooth Brush -- this is a soft rubber cap that fits over the human's finger to get the puppy used to having their teeth regularly brushed;

- Soft Bristle Brush or Comb for longer coats -- for daily grooming;

- Puppy Nail Scissors -- for trimming their toenails, and a medium-sized pair of plier style nail clippers for when they are full grown;

- One or two Soft Toys -- or wait until they come home and let them pick their own toys from the store;

- Puppy sized Treats;

- Poop Bags;

- Pee Pads;

- Bath Towels;

- Non-slip Mat for the sink or tub.

Be sure to take your Chiweenie shopping list with you when you go to your local pet store or boutique, otherwise you may forget critical items.

NOTE: if you do not already have a hairdryer, you will need to get one of these, too, so you can dry your puppy after bath time.

11. Puppy Proofing Your Home

Most puppies will be a curious bundle of energy, which means that they will get into everything within their reach.

As a responsible puppy guardian, you will want to provide a safe environment for them, which means eliminating all sources of danger, similar to what you would do for a curious toddler.

Be aware that your Chiweenie puppy will want to touch, sniff, taste, chew, investigate and closely inspect every electrical cord, every closet, every nook and cranny of your home and everything you may have left lying about on the floor.

Power cords can be found in just about every room in the home and to a teething puppy, these may look like irresistible, fun, chew toys. Make sure that you tuck all power cords securely out of your puppy's reach or enclose them inside a chew-proof PVC tube.

Kitchen -- first of all, there are many human foods that can be harmful to dogs, therefore, your kitchen should always be strictly off limits to your puppy any time you are preparing food.

Calmly send them out of the kitchen any time you are in the kitchen, and they will quickly get the idea that this area is off limits to them.

Bathroom -- bathroom cupboards and drawers or the side of a bathtub where you may leave your shaving supplies can hold many dangers for a young and curious Chiweenie puppy.

Kleenex, cotton swabs, Q-tips, toilet paper, razors, pills, soap or other materials left within your puppy's reach are an easy target that could result in an emergency visit to your veterinarian's office.

Family members need to put shampoos, soap, facial products, makeup and accessories out of reach or safely inside a cabinet or drawer.

Bedroom -- if you don't keep your shoes, slippers and clothing safely behind doors, you may find that your puppy has claimed them for their new chew toys.

Be vigilant about keeping everything in its safe place, including jewelry, hair ties, bills, coins, and other items small enough for them to swallow in containers or drawers, and secure any exposed cords or wires.

If you have children, make sure they understand that, especially while your puppy is going through their teething stage, they must keep their rooms picked up and leave nothing that could cause a choking problem to the puppy lying about on the floor or within their reach.

Living Room -- we humans spend many hours in our cozy gathering places to watch movies or play games, and often the living areas of our homes will have many items that are very enticing for a curious and teething puppy, such as books, magazines, pillows, iPods, cell phones, TV remotes and more.

You will want to keep your home free of excess clutter and remain vigilant about straightening up and putting things out of sight that could be tempting to your puppy.

Office -- we humans often spend a great deal of time in our home offices, which means that our puppy will want to be there, too, and they will be curious about all the items an office has to offer, such as cell phones, papers, books, magazines, and electrical cords.

Although your puppy might think that rubber bands or paper clips are fun to play with, allowing these items to be within your puppy's reach could end up being a fatal mistake if your puppy swallows them.

Plants: -- can be a very tempting target for your puppy's teeth, so you will want to keep them well out their reach.

If you have floor plants, they will need to be moved to a shelf or counter or placed behind a closed door until your curious fur friend grows out of the habit of putting everything in their mouth. Also keep in mind that many common houseplants are poisonous to dogs (discussed in Chapter 16).

Garage and Yard -- there are obvious as well as subtle dangers that could seriously harm or even kill a Chiweenie puppy, which can often be found in the garage or yard.

Some of these might include antifreeze, gasoline, fertilizers, rat, mice, snail and slug poison, weed killer, paint, cleaners and solvents, grass seed, bark mulch and various insecticides.

If you are storing any of these toxic substances in your garage or garden shed, make certain that you keep all such products inside a locked cabinet, or stored on high shelves that your puppy will not be able to reach. Even better, choose not to use toxic chemicals anywhere in your home or yard.

12. Puppy Hazard Home Inspection

Every conscientious puppy guardian needs to take a serious look around the home not just from the human eye level, but also from the eye level of a Chiweenie puppy.

This means literally crawling around your floors. This can be a fun exercise to ask your children to help you with.

Your puppy has a much lower vantage point that you do when standing, therefore, there may be items in your environment that could potentially be harmful to a Chiweenie puppy that a human might not notice unless you get down on the floor and take a really good look.

13. First Weeks With Your Puppy

a) The First Night

Before you go to the breeder's to pick up your new Chiweenie puppy, vacuum your floors, including all the dust bunnies under the bed.

Do a last minute check of every room to make sure that everything that could be a puppy hazard is carefully tucked away out of sight and that nothing is left on the floor or low down on shelves where a curious puppy might get into trouble.

Close most of the doors inside your home, so that there are just one or two rooms that the puppy will have access to.

You have already been shopping and have everything you need, so get out a puppy pee pad and have it at the ready when you bring your new fur friend home.

Also have your soft bed(s) in an area where you will be spending most of your time and where your puppy can easily find them.

If you have already purchased a soft toy, take the toy with you when you go to pick up your puppy.

NOTE: take either your hard-sided kennel or your soft-sided "Sherpa" travel bag (lined with pee pads) with you when going to bring your new Chiweenie puppy home, and make sure that it is securely fastened to the seat of your vehicle with the seatbelt restraint system.

Even though you will be tempted to hold your new Chiweenie puppy in your lap on the drive home, this is a very dangerous place for them to be, in case of an accident.

Place them inside their kennel or bag, which will be lined with soft towels and perhaps even a warm, towel wrapped hot water bottle (and a pee pad), and close the door.

If you have a friend who can drive for you, sit beside your puppy in the back seat, and if they cry on the way home, remind them that they are not alone with your soft, soothing voice.

Before bringing your new Chiweenie puppy inside your home, take them to the place where you want them to relieve themselves and try to wait it out long enough for them to at least go pee.

Then bring them inside your home and introduce them to the area where their food and water bowls will be kept, in case they are hungry or thirsty.

Let your puppy wander around sniffing and checking out their new surroundings and encourage them to follow you wherever you go.

Show them where the puppy pee pad is located and place it near the door where you will exit to take them outside to go potty. Many pee pads are scented to encourage a puppy to pee, and if they do, happily praise them.

Show them where their hard-sided kennel is (in your bedroom) and put them inside with the door open while you sit on the floor in front and quietly encourage them to relax inside their kennel.

Depending on the time of day when you bring your new Chiweenie puppy home for the first time, practice this kennel exercise several times throughout the day, and if they will take a little treat each time you encourage them to go inside their kennel, this will help to further encourage the behavior of them wanting to go inside.

After they have had their evening meal, take them outside approximately 20 minutes later to go to the bathroom, and when they do, make sure you are very enthusiastic with your praise and perhaps even give a little treat.

So far your Chiweenie puppy has only been allowed in several rooms of your home, as you have kept the other doors closed, so keep it this way for the first few days.

Before it's time for bed, again take your puppy outside for a very short walk to the same place where they last went potty and make sure that they go pee before bringing them back inside.

Before bed, prepare your Chiweenie puppy's hot water bottle and wrap it in a towel so that it will not be too hot for them, and place it inside their hard-sided kennel (in your bedroom).

Turn the lights down low and invite your puppy to go inside their kennel and if they seem interested, perhaps give them a soft toy to have inside with them. Let them walk into the kennel under their own steam and when they do, give them a little treat (if they are interested) and encourage them to snuggle down to sleep while you are sitting on the floor in front of the kennel.

Once they have settled down inside their kennel, close the door, go to your bed and turn all the lights off. It may help your puppy to sleep during their first night home, if you can play quiet, soothing music in the background.

If they start to cry or whine, stay calm and have compassion because this is the first time in their young life when they do not have the comfort of their mother or their litter mates.

Do not let them out of their kennel if they are crying, but rather, simply reassure them with your calm voice that they are not alone until they fall asleep.

TIP: if your bed is wide enough to accommodate your puppy's kennel, it may help them to fall asleep for the first few nights in their new kennel, if you have it beside you on top of the bed, so that you are closer to them. If there is any danger of the kennel falling off the bed during the night, do NOT do this as you will traumatize your puppy and make them afraid of their kennel.

b) The First Week

During the first week, you and your new Chiweenie puppy will be getting settled into their new routine, which will involve you getting used to your puppy's needs as they also get used to your usual schedule.

Be as consistent as possible with your waking and sleeping routine, getting up and going to bed at the same time each day, so that it will be easier for your puppy to get into the flow and routine of their new life.

First thing in the morning, remove your puppy from their kennel and take them immediately outside to relieve themselves at the place where they last went pee.

At this time, if you are teaching them to ring a doorbell to go outside, let them ring the bell before you go out the door with them, whether you are carrying them, or whether they are walking out the door on their own.

NOTE: during the first week, you may want to carry your puppy outside first thing in the morning as they may not be able to hold it for very long once waking up.

When you bring them back inside, you can let them follow you so they get used to their new leash and/or harness arrangement.

Be very careful not to drag your puppy if they stop or pull back on the leash.

TIP: if they refuse to walk on the leash, just hold the tension toward you (without pulling) while encouraging them to walk toward you, until they start to move forward again.

Now it will be time for their first feed of the day, and after they have finished eating, keep an eye on the clock, because you will want to take them outside to relieve themselves in about 20 minutes.

When your puppy is not eating or napping, they will be wanting to explore and have little play sessions with you and these times will help you bond with your puppy more and more each day.

As their new guardian, it will be your responsibility to keep a close eye on them throughout the day, so that you can notice when they need to relieve themselves and either take them to their pee pad or take them outside.

You will also need to make sure that they are eating and drinking enough throughout the day, so set regular feeding times at least three times a day.

Also set specific times in the day when you will take your puppy out for a little walk on leash and harness, so that they are not only going outside when they need to relieve themselves, but they are also learning to explore their new neighborhood with you beside them.

When your Chiweenie puppy is still very young, you will not want to walk for a long time as they will get tired easily, so keep your walks to no more than 15 or 20 minutes during your first week and if they seem tired or cold, pick them up and carry them home.

14. Common Mistakes to Avoid

a) Sleeping in Your Bed

Many of us humans make the mistake of allowing a crying puppy to sleep with them in their bed, and while this may help to calm and comfort a new puppy, it will set a dangerous precedent that can result in behavioral problems later in their life.

As well, a sleeping human body can easily crush a Chiweenie puppy.

As much as it may pull on your heart strings to hear your new Chiweenie puppy crying the first couple of night in their kennel, a little tough love at the beginning will keep them safe while helping them to learn to both love and respect you as their leader.

b) Picking Them Up at the Wrong Time

Never pick your puppy up if they display nervousness, fear or aggression (such as growling) toward an object, person or other pet, because this will be rewarding them for unbalanced behavior.

Instead, your puppy needs to be gently corrected by you, with firm and calm energy so that they learn not to react with fear or aggression.

c) Armpit Alligators

Many guardians get into the bad habit of carrying a small dog far too much. They need to be on the ground and walking on their own so that they do not become overly confident because they are always literally in the "top dog" position.

Humans who constantly carry small dogs around rather than allowing them to walk on their own can often inadvertently create what I refer to as an *"armpit alligator"* situation.

This happens when the dog becomes possessive of it's guardian who carries it everywhere, and when another adult, child or dog sees the cute little dog and approaches to say hello, the cute little dog lunges, snaps and growls.

d) Playing Too Hard or Too Long

Many humans play too hard or allow their children to play too long or too roughly with a young puppy.

You need to remember that a young puppy tires very easily and especially during the critical growing phases of their young life, they need their rest.

e) Hand Play

Always discourage your Chiweenie puppy from chewing or biting your hands, or any part of your body for that matter.

If you allow them to do this when they are puppies, they will want to continue to do so when they have strong jaws and adult teeth and this is not acceptable behavior for any breed of dog.

Do not get into the habit of playing the *"hand"* game, where you rough up the puppy and slide them across the floor with your hands, because this will teach your puppy that your hands are playthings.

When your puppy is teething, they will naturally want to chew on everything within reach, and this will include you. As cute as you might think it is, this is not an acceptable behavior and you need to gently, but firmly, discourage the habit.

A light flick with a finger on the end of a puppy nose, combined with a firm "NO" when they are trying to bite human fingers will discourage them from this activity.

f) Not Getting Used to Grooming

Not taking the time to get your Chiweenie used to a regular grooming routine, including bathing, brushing, toenail clipping and teeth brushing can lead to a lifetime of trauma for both human and dog every time these procedures must be performed.

Set aside a few minutes each day for your grooming routine.

g) Free Feeding

Free feeding means to keep food in your puppy's bowl 24/7 so that they can eat any time of the day or night, whenever they feel like it.

While free feeding a young puppy can be a good idea until they are about four or five months old, many guardians of smaller breed dogs often get into the bad habit of allowing their adult dogs to continue to eat food any time they want, by leaving food out 24/7.

This can be a serious mistake, as your Chiweenie needs to know that you are absolutely in control of their food.

If your Chiweenie does not associate the food they eat with you, they may become picky eaters or think that they are the boss, which can lead to other behavioral issues later in life.

h) Treating Them Like Fur Children

Do not get into the bad habit of treating your Chiweenie like a small fur human, because even though they may try their best to please you, and their doggy smarts could help them to succeed in most instances, not honoring them for the amazing dog they are will only cause them confusion that could lead to behavioral problems.

Remember that the one thing that your Chiweenie is the absolute best at is being a dog.

A well-balanced Chiweenie thrives on rules and boundaries, and when they understand that there is no question that you are their leader and they are your follower, they will live a contented, happy and stress-free life.

i) Distraction and Replacement

When your puppy tries to chew on your hand, foot, or your clothing, or anything else that is not fair game, you need to firmly and calmly tell them "No", and then distract them by replacing what they are not supposed to be chewing with their chew toy.

Make sure that you happily praise them every time they choose the toy to chew on.

If the puppy persists in chewing on you, remove yourself from the equation by getting up and walking away. If they are really persistent, put them inside their kennel with a favorite chew toy until they calm down.

Always praise your puppy when they stop inappropriate behavior so that they begin to understand what they can and cannot do.

15. Bonding With Your Dog

You will begin bonding with your Chiweenie puppy from the very first moment you bring them home from the breeders.

This is the time when your puppy will be the most upset and nervous, as they will no longer have the guidance, warmth and comfort of their mother or their other littermates, and you will need to take on the role of being your new puppy's center of attention.

Be patient, kind and gentle with them as they are learning you are now their new center of the universe.

Your daily interaction with your puppy during play sessions and especially your disciplined exercises, including going for walks on leash, and teaching commands and tricks, will all be wonderful bonding opportunities.

Do not make the mistake of thinking that *"bonding"* with your new puppy can only happen if you are playing or cuddling together, because the very best bonding happens when you are kindly teaching rules and boundaries, and this intelligent puppy will be most eager to learn.

What Does the Wag Mean?

It can be a mistake to automatically assume that if a dog is wagging their tail that they are happy and friendly.

When determining a dog's true intent or demeanor, you need to take into consideration the entire dog because it is entirely possible that a dog can be wagging it's tail just before it decides to take an aggressive lunge toward you.

More important in determining the emotional state of a dog is the height or positioning of the their tail.

For instance, a tail that is held parallel to the dog's back usually suggests that the dog is feeling relaxed, whereas, if the tail is held stiffly vertical, this usually means that the dog is feeling aggressive or dominant.

A tail held much lower can mean that the dog is feeling stressed, afraid, submissive or unwell and if the tail is tucked underneath the dog's body, this is most often a sign that the dog is feeling fearful and threatened by another dog or person.

Paying attention to your dog's tail can help you to know when you need to step in and make some space between your dog and another more dominant dog.

Of course, different breeds naturally carry their tails at different heights, so you will need to take this into consideration when studying your dog's tail so that you get used to their particular signals.

As well, the speed the tail is moving will also give you an idea of the mental state of the dog because the speed of the wag usually indicates how excited a dog may be.

For instance, a slow, slightly swinging wag can often mean that the dog is tentative about greeting another dog, and this is more of a questioning type of wag, whereas a fast moving tail held high can mean that a dog is about to challenge or threaten another less dominant dog.

Interestingly, two veterinarians at the University of Bari and a neuroscientist at the University of Trieste, in Italy, published a paper in which their research outlined that dogs' tails wagged more to their right side when they had positive feelings about a person or situation, and more to the left side when they were feeling negative.

While certainly a dog's tail can help us humans to understand how our dogs might be feeling, there are many other factors to take into consideration when determining your dog's state of mind.

Chapter 8: Health Problems

When considering what sort of health problems a designer or cross bred dog may be prone to, you will need to first consider the health problems associated with each breed individually.

Next, you will need to take into consideration that if the cross-bred dog is 50% one breed and 50% another that this crossing will provide the puppies with the benefits of what is called "hybrid vigor".

This means that a hybrid puppy will likely benefit physically as well as mentally from having a more varied genetic makeup than a 100% purebred puppy which could be afflicted by or susceptible to health problems that both of the purebred parents may also have.

Generally speaking, while a Chiweenie puppy will be susceptible to any type of health conditions that affect either of their parents, because the Chiweenie is half Chihuahua and half Dachshund, they will usually be genetically healthier than either of their purebred parents.

1. Chihuahua

While a healthy Chihuahua may live on average 12 to 15 years or longer, common health problems that may afflict a Chihuahua include:

a) Molleras

While this is not health problem, it is worth mentioning that the Chihuahua is the only breed of dog that is born with an *"incomplete skull"* or mollera, which is a soft spot in their skull.

This is a normal adaptation to help facilitate the passing of the dog's skull through the birth canal as well as the proper growth and development of the domed-type of forehead inherent in the breed.

The mollera, which fills in with age, will be found in nearly all Chihuahua puppies, and considerable care needs to be taken during the first six months of a puppy's life until the skull has completely formed.

b) Hydrocephalus

Water on the brain can be caused by overproduction of spinal fluid and congenitally this defect is more likely to occur in small and brachycephalic (short nosed) dogs.

As well, a tumor in the eye may cause water on the brain.

In Chihuahuas it is an inherited disease that usually becomes apparent at a few weeks of age up to about a year.

Symptoms may include lack of bladder or bowel control, sleepiness, excess vocalization, blindness, seizures, abnormally large dome-shaped head, crossed eyes, gait abnormalities, difficulty breathing, arching of the head, extension of all four legs, and coma.

Prognosis and treatment of this disease can vastly vary, with results ranging from good to poor, depending on the severity.

c) Hypoglycemia

The Chihuahua can become a picky eater, which can cause blood sugar problems.

Hypoglycemia or low blood sugar is caused by fasting too long between meals and is usually seen in puppies between 5 to 16 weeks of age.

Very tiny Chihuahua puppies are especially prone to

hypoglycemia because their lack of muscle mass makes it difficult to store glucose and regulate blood sugar.

A puppy with hypoglycemia will become drowsy, glassy-eyed, listless, shaky and uncoordinated because the brain relies upon sugar to function properly.

As well, the gums will appear very pale or grey in color and at this time the puppy may require force-feeding and also injecting fluids as they may also become dehydrated.

In extreme cases, the puppy may have a seizure or go into a coma. A puppy or dog displaying these symptoms should be given sugar in the form of corn syrup or honey and prompt veterinary treatment as prolonged hypoglycemia can cause permanent brain damage or even death.

d) Luxating Patella

This slipping kneecap condition is a common defect in Chihuahuas that may also be caused by accidentally falling or jumping from a height.

Often you will see a dog with this problem appear to be skipping down the road as they occasionally life one leg when the kneecap slips out of the patellar groove and the leg locks up.

Surgery is the treatment option for this condition, although many dogs live a relatively normal life with this defect.

e) Tracheal Collapse

Tracheal collapse or *"Brachycephalic Airway Syndrome"* is a malady that occurs in many small or toy dog breeds and is caused by a weakening of the walls of the trachea, which can become more severe with age.

The first time you hear the cough, that is similar to a goose honking, you may be quite alarmed, thinking your dog is dying as he is trying to breathe through a partially collapsed trachea.

Sometimes you can help your dog to regain full breathing by rubbing the nose, which causes them to open their mouths and relax the trachea.

Also holding the dog's ribs and giving a slight, sharp squeeze to encourage airflow can be effective.

Oftentimes the condition presents itself when the dog becomes too excited over food or play with other dogs. If the condition is severe, sometimes it can be surgically corrected.

f) Dental Issues

Often smaller breeds do not naturally lose their puppy or milk teeth without intervention from a licensed veterinarian.

It is always a good idea to keep a close watch on your puppy's teeth around the age of six or seven months to make certain that the baby teeth are gone and that the adult teeth have space to grown in.

If your puppy has not naturally lost their baby teeth, they will need to be pulled, in order to allow room for the adult teeth to grow in.

Because Chihuahuas have a small jaw they may have problems if the baby teeth do not fall out as the permanent or adult teeth grow in because the teeth become overcrowded which can cause food and plaque to build up, eventually causing bacteria to grow on the surface of the teeth, which will lead to dental disease.

It is a must to keep a close watch and brush a Chihuahua's teeth every day.

g) Intolerance to Anesthesia

The small size of the Chihuahua means that they may have a poor tolerance to anesthesia.

There is much discussion concerning the dangers of anesthesia with small dogs, and understandably, the smaller the animal, the higher the risk when administering anesthesia, or any kind of drug for that matter.

It's especially important that toy breed sizes, such as the Chihuahua, are carefully weighed so that the appropriate dose and type of anesthetic is given based on their small size.

As well, careful monitoring of blood pressure and blood glucose levels during surgical procedures is crucial for all patients, and particularly so for the tiny ones who tend to have lower body temperatures and low blood sugar (hypoglycemia).

If you are concerned about neutering or spaying a toy-sized Chiweenie, be sure to ask your veterinarian plenty of questions so that you are assured that they are up to speed with all the latest techniques that can reduce risk for smaller dogs.

Many noted health conditions can be prevented when conscientious breeders carefully screen breeding stock so that hereditary or genetic health conditions will not be passed on to the Chiweenie puppies.

2. Dachshund

While a healthy Dachshund may live to be 15 years old, some of the common health issues may include:

a) Diabetes

The level of sugar in the bloodstream is adversely affected where there is abnormal insulin production. This can lead to symptoms, such as an excessive thirst, where the dog is constantly at the water bowl, which leads to frequent urination, a dull or poor quality coat condition, and ultimately the loss of vision.

b) Hypothyroidism

This is a condition resulting from an inadequate production of thyroid hormone and is treated with medication.

Symptoms include lethargy, obesity, excessive hunger, and a coarse coat texture. Testing for thyroid malfunction is done through blood sample.

c) Intervertebral Degenerative Disk Disease

As a result of the very long back of the Dachshund, this painful condition will often affect the dog's neck and back, resulting in the dog being unwilling to exercise, and displaying symptoms of shivering which can lead to paralysis.

d) Seizures

A dog suffering from seizures, which are the result of abnormal brain activity, can display a wide variety of symptoms, including the inability to control their muscle movements, as well as bowels and bladder, excessive drooling, unsteady gait and seeming to be unaware of their surroundings.

e) Ear Infections

Ear infections may also be common due to the long narrow ear canals and long earflaps.

f) Dental Disease

Toy or Miniature Dachshunds, because of their smaller jaw, are prone to dental disease.

Again, as with all purebred canines, many noted health conditions could be prevented when conscientious breeders screen breeding stock.

In the case of a crossbred, hybrid or designer canine, such as the Chiweenie, while they may suffer from any diseases common to either purebred parent, they will usually be healthier and suffer from fewer diseases than either parent.

To ensure that the puppy you may be considering is as healthy as possible, always ask questions about whether the parents of a particular puppy have been screened and are free from the types of health problems that may be inherent in either breed.

Chiweenies are generally quite healthy small dogs and when from healthy breeding stock and well cared for can enjoy an average life expectancy of approximately 15 years, with some living even longer.

Generally speaking, while the Chiweenie could suffer from any problems inherent in either parent breed, they will usually be much healthier than either of their parents.

Fragility may also be an issue to take into consideration when considering a smaller Chiweenie, especially if the Dachshund parent is a miniature.

Many people do not realize how incredibly fragile a toy breed can be. Therefore, if the Chiweenie is bred with a Miniature Dachshund, the resulting puppies will likely be quite small dogs.

You can seriously injure or kill a small Chiweenie by stepping on them or by accidentally sitting on them when they are sleeping curled up under a warm blanket or pillow, where they frequently like to sleep.

As well, a small Chiweenie can seriously injure or even kill itself by fearlessly leaping from your arms or off the back of your sofa.

Also, a larger dog with a high prey drive can quickly grab a small Chiweenie and break his neck with one quick shake.

If you are dead set on owning a toy sized Chiweenie, this will mean that you must be constantly vigilant and keep your dog under supervision and surveillance so that you are aware of everything that is happening around your dog and can avoid any sort of harm that may befall them.

Small Chiweenies with fearless attitudes should always be kept on leash because they may place themselves into all sorts of circumstances whereby they could easily be injured when they are not under your complete control.

Also, Chiweenies are NOT suitable pets for young children, who may accidentally hurt them, or drop them.

Children are usually loud, fast moving, boisterous and oftentimes clumsy, which is a combination for danger around a small dog that might suffer all manner of injuries at the hands of a young child that meant well.

Further, most small dogs will feel overwhelmed by the loud, shrill voices and quick movements that young children can't help making with the result being that the dog may experience stress, fear and even defensive biting while it tries to defend itself from what it may believe to be a threat.

3. Allergies

One of the most common complaints discussed at the veterinarian's office when they see dogs scratching and chewing at themselves is possible allergies.

Unlike us humans, who react to allergies with nasal symptoms, when our dogs are suffering from allergies they will typically present with itchy skin or ear problems.

a) Environmental

Allergies are usually first noticed because your Chiweenie is scratching, itching, biting, licking or chewing at their skin or paws.

Just like us humans, our dogs can develop allergies to dust, chemicals, grass, mold, pollen, car exhaust, cigarette smoke, and flea and tick preparations, as well as allergies to materials, such as wool or cotton, and chemicals found in washing soap or chemicals found in cleaning products you use around your home.

Symptoms are usually seen on the stomach, inside of the legs, and at the tail or paws.

Since most allergies are seasonal, our dogs will be more affected in the spring or fall. Airborne irritants inhaled by your Chiweenie, may result in coughing, sneezing or watery eyes.

If you think that your dog may have come in contact with an environmental irritant, the best thing you can do for your dog is give them a cleansing bath, with the proper canine shampoo, followed by canine conditioner.

Remember that a Chiweenie is close to the ground, and the longer their hair, the more they resemble a duster who attracts everything they come into contact with.

b) Junk Food

"True" food allergies usually account for only about 10% of allergy problems in our canine friends.

For instance, itching, chewing and chronic ear infections are not actually caused by food allergies, but rather are the result of a suppressed immune system, which is caused by eating a low quality diet.

These types of food allergies can oftentimes be completely resolved by changing your Chiweenie's diet to a high quality food that is more easily digested.

Proper nutrition is the easiest way to prevent any food allergies.

Many dog food products contain corn, wheat and soybeans, which are common allergens. Usually it is the gluten in these foods that cause the allergic reaction.

Visit your local pet food store and educate yourself or talk with a knowledgeable representative because there's no excuse for feeding your dog a junk food diet when there are so many healthy choices now available that will help your canine companion live a long and healthy life.

Chapter 9: Daily Feeding and Care

1. Feeding Puppies

For growing puppies, a general feeding rule of thumb is to feed 10% of the puppy's present body weight or between 2% and 3% of their projected adult weight each day.

Keep in mind that high energy puppies will require extra protein to help them grow and develop into healthy adult dogs, especially during their first two years of life.

There are now many foods on the market that are formulated for all stages of a dog's life (including the puppy stage), so whether you choose one of these foods or a food specially formulated for puppies, they will need to be fed smaller meals more frequently throughout the day (3 or 4 times), until they are at least one year of age.

NOTE: choose quality sources of meat protein for healthy puppies and dogs, including beef, buffalo, chicken, duck, fish, hare, lamb, ostrich, pork, rabbit, turkey, venison, or any other source of wild meaty protein.

2. Feeding Adults

An adult dog will generally need to be fed between 2% and 3% of their body weight each day. Read the labels and avoid foods that contain a high amount of grains and other fillers. Choose foods that list high quality meat protein as the main ingredient.

TIP: grated parmesan cheese sprinkled on a Chiweenie's dinner will help to stop picky eaters from ignoring their food. To get the cheese to stick to the kibble, first mix a small amount of olive oil into the kibble, and then sprinkle with finely grated Parmesan cheese.

3. Treats

Since the creation of the first dog treat over 150 years ago the myriad of choices available on every pet store, feed store and grocery store shelf almost outnumbers those looking forward to eating them.

Today's treats are not just for making us guilty humans feel better because it makes us happy to give our fur friends something they really enjoy because today's treats are also designed to actually improve our dog's health.

Some of us humans treat our dogs, just because, others use treats for training purposes, others for health, while still others treat for a combination of reasons.

Whatever reason you choose to give treats to your Chiweenie, keep in mind that if we treat our dogs too often throughout the day, we may create a picky eater who will no longer want to eat their regular meals.

As well, if the treats we are giving are high calorie, we may be putting our dog's health in jeopardy by allowing them to become overweight.

4. Treats to Avoid

a) Rawhide

Rawhide is soaked in an ash/lye solution to remove every particle of meat, fat and hair and then further soaked in bleach to remove remaining traces of the ash/lye solution. Now that the product is no longer food, it no longer has to comply with food regulations.

While the hide is still wet it is shaped into rawhide chews, and upon drying it shrinks to approximately 1/4 of its original size.

Further, arsenic based products are often used as preservatives, and antibiotics and insecticides are added to kill bacteria that also fight against good bacteria in your dog's intestines.

The collagen fibers in the rawhide make it very tough and long lasting which makes this chew a popular choice for humans to give to their dogs because it satisfies the dog's natural urge to chew while providing many hours of quiet entertainment.

Sadly, when a dog chews a rawhide treat, they ingest many harsh chemicals and when your dog swallows a piece of rawhide, that piece now can swell up to four times its size inside your dog's stomach, which can cause anything from mild to severe gastric blockages that could become life threatening and require surgery.

b) Pig Ears

These treats are actually the ears of pigs, and while most dogs will eagerly devour them, they are extremely high in fat, which can cause stomach upsets, vomiting and diarrhea for many dogs.

Pig ears are often processed and preserved with unhealthy chemicals that discerning dog guardians will not want to feed their dogs.

As well, the ears are often quite thin and crispy and when the dog chews them pieces can break off, like chips, and can easily become stuck in a dog's throat.

While pig ears are generally not considered to be a healthy treat choice for any dog, they should be especially avoided for any dog that may be at risk of being overweight.

c) Hoof Treats

Many humans give cow, horse and pig hooves to their dogs as treats because they consider them to be *"natural"*.

The truth is that after processing these *"treats"* they retain little, if any, of their *"natural"* qualities.

Hoof treats are processed with harsh preservatives, including insecticides, lead, bleach, arsenic based products, and antibiotics to kill bacteria, that can also harm the good bacteria in your dog's intestines, and if all bacteria is not killed in these meat based products before feeding them to your dog, they could also suffer from Salmonella poisoning.

Hooves can also cause chipping or breaking of your dog's teeth as well as perforation or blockages in your dog's intestines.

5. Healthy Treats

a) Hard Treats

There are so many choices of hard, or crunchy treats available that come in many varieties of shapes, sizes and flavors, that you may have a difficult time choosing.

If your Chiweenie will eat them, hard treats will help to keep their teeth cleaner.

Whatever you do choose, be certain to read the labels and make sure that the ingredients are high quality and appropriately sized for your Chiweenie friend.

b) Soft Treats

Soft, chewy treats are also available in a wide variety of flavors, shapes and sizes for all the different needs of our fur friends and are often used for training purposes as they have a stronger smell.

c) Dental Treats

Dental treats or chews are designed with the specific purpose of helping your Chiweenie to maintain healthy teeth and gums.

They usually require intensive chewing and are often shaped with high ridges and bumps to exercise the jaw and massage gums while removing plaque build-up near the gum line.

d) Freeze-Dried and Jerky Treats

Freeze-dried and jerky treats offer a tasty morsel most dogs find irresistible as they are usually made of simple, meaty ingredients, such as liver, poultry and seafood.

These treats are usually lightweight and easy to carry around, which means they can also be great as training treats.

e) Human Food Treats

You will want to be very careful when feeding human foods to dogs as treats, because many of our foods contain additives and ingredients that could be toxic and harmful.

Be certain to choose simple, fresh foods with minimal or no processing, such as lean meat, poultry or seafood, and even if your Chiweenie will eat anything put in front of them, be aware that many common human foods, such as grapes, raisins, onions and chocolate are poisonous to dogs.

f) Training Treats

While any sort of treat can be used as an extra incentive during training sessions, soft treats are often used for training purposes because of their stronger smell and smaller sizes.

Yes, we humans love to treat our dogs, whether for helping to teach the new puppy to go pee outside, teaching the adolescent dog new commands, for trick training, for general good behavior, or for no reason at all, other than that they just gave us the *"look"*.

Generally, the treats you feed your dog should not make up more than approximately 10% of their daily food intake, so make sure the treats you choose are high quality, so that you can help to keep your Chiweenie both happy and healthy.

6. Choosing the Right Food

In order to choose the right food for your Chiweenie, first, it's important to understand a little bit about canine physiology and what Mother Nature intended when she created our fur friends.

More than 230 years ago, in 1785, the English Sportman's dictionary described the best diet for a dog's health in an article entitled *"Dog"*.

This article indicated that the best food for a dog was something called *"Greaves"*, described as *"the sediment of melted tallow. It is made into cakes for dogs' food. In Scotland and parts of the US it is called cracklings."*

Out of the meager beginning of the first commercially made dog food has sprung a massively lucrative and vastly confusing industry that has only recently begun to evolve beyond those early days of feeding our dogs the dregs of human leftovers because it was cheap and convenient for us humans.

Even today, the majority of dog food choices have far more to do with being convenient for humans to store and serve than it does with being a diet truly designed to be a nutritionally balanced, healthy food choice for a canine.

The dog food industry is big business and as such, because there are now almost limitless choices, there is much confusion and endless debate when it comes to answering the question, *"What is the best food for my dog?"*

Educating yourself, by talking to experts and reading everything you can find on the subject, plus taking into consideration several relevant factors, will help to answer the dog food question for you and your dog.

For instance, where you live may dictate what sorts of foods you have access to. Other factors to consider will include the particular requirements of your dog, such as their age, energy and activity levels.

Next will be expense, time and quality. While we all want to give our dogs the best food possible, many humans lead very busy lives and cannot, for instance, prepare their own dog food, but still want to feed a high quality diet that fits within their budget.

However, perhaps most important when choosing an appropriate diet for our dogs, is learning to be more observant of Mother Nature's design and taking a closer look at our dog's teeth, jaws and digestive tract.

While humans are herbivores who derive energy from eating plants, our canine companions are carnivores, which means that they derive their energy and nutrient requirements from eating a diet consisting mainly or exclusively of the flesh of animal tissues (in other words, meat).

a) The Canine Teeth

The first part of your dog you will want to take a good look at when considering what to feed will be their teeth.

Unlike humans, who are equipped with wide, flat molars for grinding grains, vegetables and other plant-based materials, canine teeth are all pointed because they are designed to rip, shred and tear into animal meat and bone.

b) The Canine Jaw

Another obvious consideration when choosing an appropriate food source for our fur friends, is the fact that every canine is born equipped with powerful jaws and neck muscles for the specific purpose of being able to pull down and tear apart their hunted prey.

The structure of the jaw of every canine is such that it opens widely to hold large pieces of meat and bone, while the actual mechanics of a dog's jaw permits only vertical (up and down) movement that is designed for crushing.

c) The Canine Digestive Tract

A dog's digestive tract is short and simple and designed to move their natural choice of food (hide, meat and bone) quickly through their systems.

Vegetables and plant matter require more time to break down in the gastrointestinal tract, which in turn, requires a more complex digestive system than the canine body is equipped with.

The canine digestive system is simply unable to break down vegetable matter, which is why whole vegetables look pretty much the same going into your dog as they do coming out the other end.

Given the choice, most dogs would never choose to eat plants or vegetables and fruits over meat, however, we humans continue to feed them a kibble based diet that contains high amounts of vegetables, fruits and grains and low amounts of meat.

Plus, in order to get our dogs to eat fruits, vegetables and grains we usually have to flavor the food with meat or meat by-products.

How much healthier and long lived might our beloved fur friends be if, instead of largely ignoring nature's design for our canine companions, we chose to feed them whole, unprocessed, species-appropriate food?

With many hundreds of dog food brands to choose from, it's no wonder we humans are confused about what to feed our dogs to help them live long and healthy lives.

Following are some suggestions and questions that may help you choose a dog food company that you can feel comfortable with:

- how long have they have been in business?
- is dog food their main industry?
- are they dedicated to their brand?
- are they easily accessible?
- do they honestly answer your questions?
- do they have a good Company Safety Standard?
- do they set higher standards?
- read the ingredients - where did they come from?
- are the ingredients something you would eat?
- are the ingredients farmed locally?
- was it cooked using standards you would trust?
- is the company certified under human food or organic guidelines?

Whatever you decide to feed your Chiweenie, keep in mind that, just as too much wheat, other grains and other fillers in our human diet is having detrimental effects on our human health, the same can be very true for our best fur friends.

Our dogs are also suffering from many of the same life threatening diseases that are rampant in our human society (heart disease, cancer) as a direct result of consuming a diet high in genetically altered, impure, processed and packaged foods.

7. The Raw Diet

While some of us believe we are killing ourselves as well as our dogs with processed foods, others believe that there are dangers in feeding raw foods.

Those who are raw feeding advocates believe that the ideal diet for their dog is one which would be very similar to what a dog living in the wild would have access to hunting or foraging, and these canine guardians are often opposed to feeding their dog any sort of commercially manufactured pet foods, because they consider them to be poor substitutes.

On the other hand, those opposed to feeding their dogs a raw or biologically appropriate raw food diet, believe that the risks associated with food-borne illnesses during the handling and feeding of raw meats outweigh the purported benefits.

Interestingly, even though the United States Food and Drug Administration (FDA) states that they do not advocate a raw diet for dogs, they do advise for those who wish to take this route, that following basic hygiene guidelines for handling raw meat can minimize any associated risks.

Further, high pressure pasteurization (HPP), which is high pressure, water based technology for killing bacteria, is USDA-approved for use on organic and natural food products, and is being utilized by many commercial raw pet food manufacturers.

Interestingly, raw meats purchased at your local grocery store contain a much higher level of acceptable bacteria than raw food produced for dogs because the meat purchased for human consumption is supposed to be cooked, which will kill any bacteria that might be present.

This means that canine guardians feeding their dogs a raw food diet can be quite certain that commercially prepared raw foods sold in pet stores will be safer than raw meats purchased in grocery stores.

Many guardians of high energy, working breed dogs will agree that their dogs thrive on a raw or BARF (Biologically Appropriate Raw Food) diet and strongly believe that the potential benefits of feeding a raw dog food diet are many, including:

- healthy, shiny coats
- decreased shedding
- fewer allergy problems
- healthier skin
- cleaner teeth
- fresher breath
- higher energy levels
- improved digestion
- smaller stools
- strengthened immune system
- increased mobility in arthritic pets
- increase or improvement in overall health

All dogs, of every size, whether working breed or companion dogs are amazing athletes in their own right, therefore every dog deserves to be fed the best food available.

A raw diet is a direct evolution of what dogs ate before they became our domesticated pets and we turned toward commercially prepared, easy to serve dry dog food that required no special storage or preparation.

The BARF diet is all about feeding our dogs what they are designed to eat by returning them to their wild, evolutionary diet.

8. The Dehydrated Diet

Dehydrated dog food comes in both raw meat and cooked meat

forms and these foods are usually air dried to reduce moisture to the level where bacterial growth is inhibited.

The appearance of de-hydrated dog food is very similar to dry kibble and the typical feeding methods include adding warm water before serving, which makes this type of diet both healthy for our dogs and convenient for us to serve.

Dehydrated recipes are made from minimally processed fresh whole foods to create a healthy and nutritionally balanced meal that will meet or exceed the dietary requirements of a healthy canine.

Dehydrating removes only the moisture from the fresh ingredients, which usually means that because the food has not already been cooked at a high temperature, more of the overall nutrition is retained.

A de-hydrated diet is a convenient way to feed your dog a nutritious diet because all you have to do is add warm water, and wait five minutes while the food re-hydrates so your Chiweenie can enjoy a warm meal.

9. The Kibble Diet

While many canine guardians are starting to take a closer look at the food choices they are making for their furry companions, there is no mistaking that the convenience and relative economy of dry dog food kibble, that had its beginnings in the 1940's, continues to be the most popular pet food choice for most dog friendly humans.

Some 75 years later, the massive pet food industry offers up a confusingly large number of choices with hundreds of different manufacturers and brand names lining the shelves of veterinarian offices, grocery stores and pet food aisles.

While feeding a high quality bagged kibble diet that has been flavored to appeal to dogs and supplemented with vegetables and fruits to appeal to humans, may keep most every Chiweenie companion happy and relatively healthy, you will ultimately need to decide whether this is the best diet for them.

10. The Right Bowl

Following is a brief description of the different categories and types of dog bowls that would be appropriate choices for your Chiweenie's particular needs.

Automatic Watering Bowls: are standard dog bowls (often made out of plastic) that are attached to a reservoir container, which is designed to keep water constantly available to your dog as long as there is water remaining in the storage compartment.

Ceramic/Stoneware Bowls: an excellent choice for those who like options in personality, color and shape.

Elevated Bowls: raised dining table dog bowls are a tidy and classy choice that will make your dog's dinner time a more comfortable experience while getting the bowls off the floor.

No Skid Bowls: are for dogs that push their bowls across the floor when eating. A non-skid dog bowl will help keep the feed bowl where you put it.

No Tip Bowls: are designed to prevent the messy type of doggy eater from flipping over their dinner or water bowls.

Stainless Steel Bowls: are as close to indestructible as a bowl can be, plus they are sanitary, easy to clean and water stays cooler for a longer period of time in a stainless bowl.

Wooden Bowls: for those humans concerned about stylish home decor, wooden dog bowl dining stations are beautiful pieces of furniture unto themselves that can enhance your home decor.

Travel Bowls: are a convenient, practical and handy addition for every canine travel kit.

Consider a space saving, collapsible dog bowl, made out of hygienic, renewable bamboo that comes in fun colors and different sizes, making it perfect for every travel bowl needs.

If you would like to learn more about all the many dog bowl choices available, visit DogBowlForYourDog.com, which is a comprehensive, one-stop website dedicated to explaining the ins and outs of every food bowl imaginable and helping you find the perfect bowl for all your Chiweenie's needs.

11. Exercise

All of our canine companions are amazing, natural athletes and because of this, they need daily exercise to stay fit, happy and healthy.

The energetic Chiweenie is no exception to this rule. Every Chiweenie will love going for walks or engaging in any manner of canine sport with their guardian several times every day.

As well, taking your Chiweenie for a disciplined walk, where they are on leash and calmly walking beside you without straining on the leash or trying to lead you, will reinforce that you are the boss and they are the follower.

Any type of disciplined exercise you can engage in with your Chiweenie will help to exercise both their body and their mind and will burn off daily energy reserves so that your Chiweenie will be a happy and contented companion.

If you find that your Chiweenie is being a pest by chewing inappropriate items around the home or being demanding of your time, or especially unruly when visitors come to call, this is likely because they are not being challenged enough or exercised often enough, or long enough each day to drain out their daily pent up energy.

A healthy, adult Chiweenie will thrive when being walked several times each day and will enjoy the challenge of being engaged in other forms of disciplined activity, such as Obedience, Rally, Freestyle Dance or Agility.

12. Playtime

Every dog needs some regular playtime each day, and this is even more important with an active breed, such as the Chiweenie, who will be your loving, energetic companion.

While every Chiweenie will be different with respect to what types of games they may enjoy, most Chiweenie's will enjoy a game of fetch with a ball or chasing a Frisbee, and some may even enjoy swimming to retrieve a stick.

A fun game of *"Search"*, where you ask your Chiweenie to "Sit/Stay" while you hide a favorite treat that they then have to find, will appeal to the Chiweenie's ancient hunting instincts.

After a disciplined walk with your Chiweenie, they will also enjoy being given the opportunity for some off leash freedom to run. play and socialize with other similar sized dogs.

13. Daily Grooming

Daily grooming is a must for any healthy Chiweenie.

Get into the routine of spending at least 15 minutes each day brushing or combing your Chiweenie, checking their nails and brushing their teeth.

14. Safe Traveling

Far too many canine guardians do nothing to protect their companions when traveling with them inside their vehicles.

According to a 2011 American Automobile Association study, only about 16% of dog owners restrain their pets when riding in a vehicle, and of those who are trying, many are not properly securing their beloved pets.

That leaves 84% of people who let their dogs roam freely about the inside of their vehicles, leaving them at serious risk of being injured or killed in an automobile accident.

For example, when a vehicle traveling at only 30 miles per hour (48.28 kilometers per hour) is involved in an accident, a small, ten pound (4.54 kg), unrestrained dog will be subjected to approximately 300 pounds force (136 kilogram-force), which is certainly enough to seriously injure or kill a Chiweenie.

There is no denying that dogs that are not properly restrained become projectiles in any sort of vehicle crash.

As well, many drivers permit their smaller dogs to sit on their lap when driving, which is not only distracting to the driver, but if involved in an accident, the vehicle's airbags will deploy at 300 mph (482.8 kilometers per hour) which can easily snap the neck of a small dog.

a) Faulty Restraints

Many dog lovers may be laboring under the misconception that they are doing the right thing by buckling their canine companions into a safety harness because they are unaware that many of these dog harnesses that are supposed to keep furry passengers safe have a 100% failure rate.

Statistics collected by the Center for Pet Safety (CPS) have shown that every popular restraint tested with dog dummies, traveling at a sedate 30 mph (48.28 km/h), not only failed, but also indicated that serious injuries or deaths were highly likely.

Most restraints that were tested in the CPS study allowed dogs to easily become flying projectiles during vehicle accidents because the harnesses were simply not strong enough to keep them in their seats, and in many cases the restraints could actually choke the dog during a crash.

When the MGA Research Corporation carried out a pilot study for The Center for Pet Safety (CPS), in which they tested 12 major brands of pet harnesses, the results indicated a **100% failure rate**.

According to the American Kennel Club, these safety harness tests were carried out using the average weights of the ten most popular breeds of dogs, including the Labrador Retriever, the German Shepherd, the Golden Retriever, the Beagle, the Bulldog, the Chihuahua, the Boxer, the Dachshund, the Rottweiler and the Dachshund.

The founder and chairman of CPS, believes that,

"Saying that these products prevent your pet from becoming a projectile in an accident is a potentially misleading statement."

Law enforcement agencies, safety advocates, insurance companies, and concerned dog owners need to keep pressing for the development of a standard for dog safety equipment, to insist that all such equipment pass a government regulated crash test before being sold as safe for travel.

The safest travel arrangement for any dog is to secure them inside a travel bag or kennel, followed by finding a safety restraint that is crash and strength tested and certified to be safe for your dog.

b) Kennels

If you opt to contain your best friend inside a kennel, crate or travel bag, you absolutely must make sure that the kennel or bag is very securely attached with the vehicle's seatbelt system or even better, with special tie downs that are bolted to the floor of the vehicle.

A small dog kennel or crate will easily fit on the back seat of most vehicles and can be secured with the vehicle's restraint system.

A Chiweenie riding inside a kennel, crate or travel bag inside your vehicle will have the best protection in the case of a rollover accident.

There is at least one manufacturer of a travel bag restraint system, called 'Sleepypod™", designed for pets up to 15 pounds (6.8 kg) that goes the extra mile for safety and actually puts its own products through the child safety seat test.

All four models of the Sleepypod™ have passed the 30 mph (48.28 km/h) crash test.

c) Harness Restraints

The Kurgo Tru-Fit Smart harness has been crash and strength tested and with its steel nesting buckles has a tensile strength tested to withstand a force of 2250 pounds (1020 kilogram-force). The crash test videos of this product depict a 35-pound (15.9 kilogram) dummy dog traveling at 30 miles per hour (48.28 km/h), recorded at an accredited University test facility.

The Ruff Rider Roadie® harness successfully passed the preliminary test criteria for both dynamic and static load limits.

Ruff Rider's only product is the Roadie® travel restraint which was invented by dog owner, Carl Goldberg, after his pet was ejected through the front windshield of his vehicle during a minor collision.

The design of the Roadie® is so unique that it was awarded three (3) patents, and over the past 20 years Roadie® has helped protect many dogs during vehicle accidents.

Sleepypod™ manufactures a safety harness called *"Clickit Utility"* that has a #1 safety rating. Apparently, this harness is the first dog safety harness to incorporate three-points of attachment to better absorb force caused in a front end collision by effectively dissipating energy while keeping the dog in the car seat during an impact (patents pending).

The Clickit Utility harness can also be used in the cargo area and includes a d-ring on the back of the vest so it can be used as a walking harness.

Keep your Chiweenie safe when traveling in your vehicle. Do your research and either transport your dog inside a kennel, or find a safety harness that is both strength tested and certified to be able to keep your Chiweenie safe in the event of an accident.

d) Sherpa for Small Dogs

"Sherpa" is a name that refers to a soft-sided dog carrier with zippered pockets for carrying important papers, treats, baggies, etc., that has mesh sides for superior ventilation.

While there is an actual "Sherpa" brand name, this name has become synonymous with any type of soft-sided carrier bag.

The Sherpa bag has handles as well as a shoulder strap and some even have wheels, so your Chiweenie puppy or dog will be able to safely travel anywhere in style and comfort.

The smaller Chiweenie will be the perfect candidate for learning to travel about inside a Sherpa or soft-sided travel bag, such as the Sleepypod™.

When they are young puppies, get them used to Sherpa travel by putting them inside their bag every time they need to go outside, and before you bring them back inside. When you do this, a Chiweenie puppy will very quickly learn to love scooting into their bag because they associate it with the fun activity of going outside with you.

Once your Chiweenie puppy becomes used to Sherpa travel, it will be very easy for them to travel with you wherever you go, including public transportation (buses), boats, planes and vehicles, and the best way to start them getting used to this idea is as soon as you bring your new puppy home.

Every time you go to your vehicle, put your Chiweenie inside their Sherpa bag and pretty soon they will associate fun adventures with the Sherpa and will not hesitate to quickly hop inside.

"Sleepypod™" manufactures various styles of higher end travel bags for small dogs, such as the Chiweenie, and puts their bags through rigorous crash testing to ensure they are totally safe.

Although these bags are considerably more costly than many other canine travel bags, you will have peace of mind knowing that your Chiweenie will always be safe when riding inside one.

e) Air Travel

A smaller Chiweenie, can be *"carry on baggage"* if the carrier conforms to the airline regulations, which state that a pet carrier must be able to fit under the seat in front of you. Most soft carriers are airline approved and under seat dimensions are generally as follows:

Window Seat: 19" L x 14" W x 8.25" H
[48.26 cm L x 35.56 cm W x 20.955 cm H]
Middle Seat: 19" L x 19" W x 8.25" H
[48.26 cm L x 48.26 cm W x 20.955 cm H]
Aisle Seat: 19" L x 14" W x 8.25" H
[48.26 cm L x 35.56 cm W x 20.955 cm H]

For in-cabin travel by plane, your dog must be able to stand up and turn around comfortably inside the bag. Airlines also require an absorbent liner in the bag, which could be a pee pad, an old towel, a favorite blanket, or a cozy, faux lambskin liner.

Many styles of canine carrier bags are officially approved for airline travel, and when you make your flight reservations, don't forget to reserve for your Chiweenie as well because there is generally a small charge for in-cabin travel and some airlines will only permit a certain number of canine travelers per flight.

Chapter 10: House Training

1. Human Training

House training, house breaking, or *"potty"* training, is a critical first step in the education of any new puppy, and the first part of a successful process is training the human guardian.

When you bring home your new Chiweenie puppy, they will be relying upon your guidance to teach them what they need to learn.

When you provide your puppy with your consistent patience and understanding, they are capable of learning rules at a very early age, and house training is no different, especially since it's all about establishing a regular routine.

Potty training a new puppy takes time and patience — how much time depends entirely upon you.

Check in with yourself and make sure your energy remains consistently calm and patient and that you exercise plenty of compassion and understanding while you help your new puppy learn their new bathroom rules.

Chiweenie puppies and dogs flourish with routines and happily, so do humans, therefore, the first step is to establish a daily routine that will work well for both canine and human alike.

For instance, depending upon the age of your Chiweenie puppy, make a plan to take them out for a bathroom break every two hours and stick to it because while you are in the beginning stages of potty training, the more vigilant and consistent you can be, the quicker and more successful your results will be.

Generally speaking, while your puppy is still growing, a young puppy can hold it approximately one hour for every month of their age.

This means that if your 2-month-old puppy has been happily snoozing for a couple of hours, as soon as they wake up, they will need to go outside.

Some of the first indications or signs that your puppy needs to be taken outside to relieve themselves will be when you see them:

- sniffing around
- circling
- looking for the door
- whining, crying or barking
- acting agitated

It will be important to always take your Chiweenie puppy out first thing every morning, and immediately after they wake up from a nap as well as soon after they have finished eating a meal or having a big drink of water.

Also, your happy praise goes a long way toward encouraging and reinforcing future success when your Chiweenie puppy makes the right decisions, so let them know you are happy when they do their business in the right place.

Initially, treats can be a good way to reinforce how pleased you are that your puppy is learning to go potty in the right place. Slowly treats can be removed and replaced with your happy praise.

Next, now that you have a new puppy in your life, you will want to be flexible with respect to adapting your schedule to meet the requirements that will help to quickly teach your Chiweenie puppy their new bathroom routine.

This means not leaving your puppy alone for endless hours at a time because firstly, they are sensitive pack animals that need companionship and your direction at all times, plus long periods alone will result in the disruption of the potty training schedule you have worked hard to establish.

If you have no choice but to leave your puppy alone for many hours, make sure that you place them in a paper lined room or pen where they can relieve themselves without destroying your favorite carpet or new hardwood flooring.

Remember, your Chiweenie is a growing puppy with a bladder and bowels that they do not yet have complete control over and you will have a much happier time and better success if you simply train yourself to pay attention to when your young companion is showing signs of needing to relieve themselves.

2. Bell Training

A very easy way to introduce your new Chiweenie puppy to house training is to begin by teaching them how to ring a doorbell whenever they need to go outside.

Ringing a doorbell is not only a convenient alert system for both you and your Chiweenie puppy or dog, your visitors will be most impressed by how smart your Chiweenie is.

A further benefit of training your puppy to ring a bell is that you will not have to listen to your puppy or dog whining, barking or howling to be let out, and your door will not become scratched up from their nails.

Unless you prefer to purchase an already manufactured doggy doorbell or system, take a trip to your local novelty store and purchase a small bell that has a nice, loud ring.

Attach the bell to a piece of ribbon or string and hang it from a door handle or tape it to a door sill near the door where you will be taking your puppy out when they need to relieve themselves. The string will need to be long enough so that your Chiweenie puppy can easily reach the bell with their nose or a paw.

Next, each time you take your puppy out to go potty, say the word *"Out"*, and use their paw or their nose to ring the bell. Praise them for this *"trick"* and immediately take them outside.

The only down side to teaching your Chiweenie puppy or dog to ring a bell when they want to go outside, is that even if they don't actually have to go out to relieve themselves, but just want to go outside because they are bored, you will still have to take them out every time they ring the bell.

There are many types and styles of *"gotta' go"* commercially manufactured bells you could choose, ranging from the elegant **"Poochie Bells™"** that hang from a doorknob, the simple **"Tell Bell™"** that sits on the floor, or various high tech door chime systems that function much like a doggy intercom system where they push a pad with their paw and it rings a bell.

Whatever doorbell system you choose for your Chiweenie puppy, once they are trained, this type of an alert system is an easy way to eliminate accidents in the home.

3. Kennel Training

Kennel training is always a good idea for any puppy early in their education, because it can be utilized for many different situations, including keeping them safe while traveling inside a vehicle and being a very helpful tool for house training.

When purchasing a kennel for your Chiweenie puppy, always buy a kennel that will be the correct size for your puppy once they become an adult.

The kennel will be the correct size if an adult Chiweenie can stand up and easily turn around inside their kennel.

When you train your Chiweenie puppy to accept sleeping in their own kennel at nighttime, this will also help to accelerate their potty training, because no puppy or dog wants to relieve themselves where they sleep, which means that they will hold their bladder and bowels as long as they possibly can.

Always be kind and compassionate and remember that a puppy will be able to hold it approximately one hour for every month of their age.

Generally, a Chiweenie puppy that is three months old will be able to hold it for approximately three hours, unless they just ate a meal or had a big drink of water.

Be watchful and consistent so that you learn your Chiweenie puppy's body language, which will alert you to when it's time for them to go outside.

Presenting them with familiar scents, by taking them to the same spot in the yard or the same street corner, will help to remind and encourage them that they are outside to relieve themselves.

Use a voice cue to remind your puppy why they are outside, such as *"go pee"* and always remember to praise them every time they relieve themselves in the right place so that they quickly understand what you expect of them and will learn to *"go"* on cue.

4. Exercise Pen Training

The exercise pen is a transition from kennel only training and will be helpful for those times when you may have to leave your Chiweenie puppy for more hours than they can reasonably be expected to hold it.

During those times when you must be away from the home for several hours, it's time to introduce your Chiweenie puppy to an exercise pen.

Exercise pens are usually constructed of wire sections that you can put together in whatever shape you desire, and the pen needs to be large enough to hold your puppy's kennel inside one half of the pen, while the other half will be lined with newspapers or pee pads.

Place your Chiweenie puppy's food and water dishes next to the kennel and leave the kennel door open, so they can wander in and out whenever they wish, to eat or drink or go to the papers or pads if they need to relieve themselves.

Your puppy will be contained in a small area of your home while you are away and because they are already used to sleeping inside their kennel, they will not want to relieve themselves inside the area where they sleep. Therefore, your Chiweenie puppy will naturally go to the other half of the pen to relieve themselves on the newspapers or pee pads.

This method will help train your puppy to be quickly "paper" trained when you must leave them alone for a few hours.

5. Puppy Apartment™ Training

A similar and more costly alternative, the *Puppy Apartment*™ is a step up from the exercise pen training system that makes the process of crate or pen training even easier on both humans and puppies.

The Puppy Apartment™ works well in a variety of situations, whether you're at home and unable to pay close attention to your Chiweenie puppy's needs, whether you must be away from the home for a few hours or during the evening when everyone is asleep and you don't particularly want to get up at 3:00 a.m. to take your Chiweenie puppy out to go pee.

The Puppy Apartment™ is an innovation that is convenient for both puppy and human alike.

What makes this system so effective is the patent pending dividing wall with a door leading to the other side, all inside the pen.

One side of the Puppy Apartment™ is where the puppy's bed is located and the other side (through the doorway) is the bathroom area that is lined with pee pads.

With the bathroom right next door, your Chiweenie puppy or dog can take a bathroom break whenever they wish, without the need to alert family members to let them out.

This one bedroom, one bathroom system, which is a combination of the kennel/training pen, is a great alternative for helping to eliminate the stress of worrying about always keeping a watchful eye on your puppy or getting up during the night to take them outside every few hours to help them avoid making mistakes.

According to Modern Puppies...

> *"The Puppy Apartment™ takes the MESSY out of paper training, the ODORS AND HASSLES out of artificial grass training, MISSING THE MARK out of potty pad training and HAVING TO HOLD IT out of crate training. House training a puppy has never been faster or easier!*
>
> *The Puppy Apartment™ has taken all the benefits of the most popular potty training methods and combined them into one magical device and potty training system. This device and system has revolutionized how modern puppies are potty trained!"*

Manufactured in the United States, this product ships directly from the California supplier (Modern Puppies).

Pricing of the Puppy Apartment™ begins at $138. USD (£83.37) and is only available online at Modern Puppies.

6. Free Training

If you would rather not confine your young Chiweenie puppy to one or two rooms in your home, and will be allowing them to freely range about your home anywhere they wish during the day, this is considered free training.

When free house training your Chiweenie puppy, you will need to closely watch your puppy's activities all day long so that you can be aware of the *"signs"* that will indicate when they need to go outside to relieve themselves.

For instance, circling and sniffing is a sure sign that they are looking for a place to do their business.

Never get upset or scold a puppy for having an accident inside the home, because this will result in teaching your puppy to be afraid of you and to only relieve themselves in secret places or when you're not watching.

If you catch your Chiweenie puppy making a mistake, all that is necessary is for you to calmly say *"No"*, and quickly scoop them up and take them outside or to their indoor bathroom area.

From your sensitive puppy's point of view, yelling or screaming when they make a potty mistake, will be understood by your puppy or dog as unstable energy being displayed by the person who is supposed to be their leader. This type of unstable behavior will only teach your puppy to fear and disrespect you.

When you are vigilant, the Chiweenie should not a difficult puppy to housebreak and they will generally do very well when you start them off with *"puppy pee pads"* that you will move closer and closer to the same door that you always use when taking them outside. This way they will quickly learn to associate going to this door when they need to relieve themselves.

When you pay close attention to your Chiweenie puppy's sleeping, eating, drinking and playing habits, you will quickly learn their body language so that you are able to predict when they might need to relieve themselves.

Your Chiweenie puppy will always need to relieve themselves first thing in the morning, as soon as they wake up from a nap, approximately 20 minutes after they finish eating a meal, after they have finished a play session, and of course, before they go to bed at night.

It's important to have compassion during this house training time in your young Chiweenie's life so that their education will be as stress-free as possible.

It's also important to be vigilant because how well you pay attention will minimize the opportunities your puppy may have for making a bathroom mistake in the first place, and the fewer mistakes they make, the sooner your Chiweenie puppy will be house trained.

7. Mistakes Happen

Remember that a dog's sense of smell is at least 2,000 times more sensitive that our human sense of smell.

As a result of your Chiweenie puppy's superior sense of smell, it will be very important to effectively remove all odors from house training accidents, because otherwise, your Chiweenie puppy will be attracted by the smell to the place where they may have had a previous accident, and will want to do their business there again and again.

While there are many products that are supposed to remove odors and stains, many of these are not very effective. You want a professional grade cleaner that will not just mask one odor with another scent, you want a product that will completely neutralize odors.

TIP: go to RemoveUrineOdors.com and order yourself some *"SUN"* and/or *"Max Enzyme"* because these products contain professional-strength odor neutralizers and urine digesters that bind to and completely absorb odors on any type of surface.

8. Electronic Training Devices

Generally speaking, positive training methods are far more effective than using devices that involve negative stimulation.

Further, unless you are training a Chiweenie to hunt badgers or rabbits, using electronic devices is usually a excuse for a lazy human who will not take the time to properly train their dog by teaching them rules and boundaries which leads to respect and an attentive follower.

When you do not provide your Chiweenie (or any dog) with a consistent leadership role that teaches your dog to trust, respect and listen to you in all circumstances, you will inevitably experience behavioral issues.

Electronic training devices such as e-collars, spray collars or electronic fencing all rely upon negative, painful or stressful reinforcement, which can easily cause a sensitive breed, like the Chiweenie, to become nervous or live a life of fear.

For instance, a dog simply cannot understand the principles of "invisible" boundaries, and therefore, should never be subjected to the confusion of the punishment that occurs when walking across an invisible line within their own home territory.

Dogs naturally understand the positive training methods of receiving a reward, which is not only much more efficient and effective when teaching boundaries, rewards are far kinder, and create a much stronger bond with your dog.

a) The Truth About Shock Collars

First of all, it would have to be an extremely rare situation in which it would be necessary or recommended that you use a shock collar on a small Chiweenie as these devices are usually only employed in extreme situations, and generally for much larger breeds who could seriously harm someone.

The use of remote, electronic, shock or *"e-collars"* is at best a controversial subject that can quickly escalate into heated arguments.

In certain, rare circumstances, and when used correctly, the e-collar can be a helpful training tool that could actually save a dog's life if they are acting out in dangerous ways.

An e-collar would generally be utilized in a circumstance where a larger breed of dog has access to free range over a large property, resulting in difficulties getting their attention from a distance if they become distracted by other animals or smells.

Many dogs that not been properly trained from a young age also learn that when they are off leash and out of your immediate reach that they can choose to ignore your commands, bark their heads off, terrorize the neighbors or chase wildlife.

All of these situations are generally not activities that a Chiweenie would have the slightest interest in because they love being at home with their humans.

Generally e-collars can be effective training tools for working breed herding or hunting or tracking dogs.

In these types of circumstances a remote training collar can be an effective training device for reinforcing verbal commands from a great distance, such as "Come", "Sit" or "Stay".

Finally, electronic collars can be used as a last resort to help teach a dog not to engage in a dangerous behavior that could result in them being seriously harmed or even killed.

b) Electronic Fencing

Honestly, there are far more reasons NOT to install an electronic fence as a means of keeping your dog inside your yard, than there are good reasons for considering one.

For instance, a dog whose yard is surrounded by an electronic fence can quite easily develop fear, aggression, or both, directed toward what they may believe is the cause of the shock they are receiving.

As a result, installing an electronic fence may cause your Chiweenie to become aggressive toward cats, other dogs, other humans, other wildlife, children riding by on bikes or skateboards, the mail carrier, or the dog next door.

As well, a dog that receives a fright, or in excitement forgets about the shock they are going to receive, may run through an electronic fence and then be too frightened or stressed to come back home because it means that they must pass through the painful barrier again.

Further, it is actually possible that electronic fencing may encourage a dog to escape the yard simply because they associate their yard with pain. This feeling can be reinforced if a dog escapes the electronic yard and then is again punished by the shock when they attempt to come home.

Another factor to keep in mind with respect to electronic fencing is that other dogs or teasing children can freely enter the yard and torment or attack your dog, and a thief bent on stealing your Chiweenie will be able to do so with ease.

The absolute best way to keep your dog safe in their own yard, while helping to establish your role as guardian and leader, is to be out there with them while they are on leash, and to only permit them freedom in your yard under your close supervision.

Chapter 11: Medical Care & Safety

1. Choosing a Veterinarian

A consideration to keep in mind when choosing a veterinarian clinic will be that some clinics specialize in caring for smaller pets, and some specialize in larger animal care, while still others have a wide ranging area of expertise and will care for all animals, including livestock and reptiles.

Choosing a clinic will be a personal decision, however, since the Chiweenie is considered a smaller breed of dog, your dog's needs may be better served by choosing a clinic that specializes in the care of smaller pets.

Choosing a good veterinary clinic will be very similar to choosing the right health care clinic or doctor for your own personal health because you want to ensure that your Chiweenie puppy receives the quality care they deserve.

Begin your search by asking other dog owners where they take their fur friends and whether they are happy with the service they receive.

If you don't know anyone to ask, visit the local pet store in your area as they should be able to provide you with references and local listings of pet care clinics.

Next, check online, because a good pet clinic will have an active website up and running that will list details of all the services they provide along with an overview of all staff members, their education and qualifications.

Once you've narrowed your search, it's time to personally visit the clinics you may be interested in, as this will be a good opportunity for you to visually inspect the facility, interact with the staff and perhaps meet the veterinarians face to face.

Of course, it's not just you who needs to feel comfortable with the clinic chosen and those working there. Your puppy needs to feel comfortable, too, and this is where visiting a clinic and interacting with the staff and veterinarians will provide you with an idea of their experience and expertise in handling your puppy.

If your puppy is comfortable with them, then you will be much more likely to trust that they will be providing the best care for your puppy who will need to receive all their vaccinations and yearly check-ups, and eventually be spayed or neutered.

It's also a good idea to take your puppy into your chosen clinic several times before they actually need to be there for any treatment, so that they are not fearful of the new smells and unfamiliar surroundings.

2. Neutering and Spaying

While it can sometimes be difficult to find the definitive answer when asking when is the best time to neuter or spay your young Chiweenie, because there are varying opinions on this topic, one thing that most veterinarians do agree on is that earlier spaying or neutering, between 4 and 6 months of age, is a better choice than waiting.

Spaying or neutering surgeries are carried out under general anesthesia, and as more dogs are being neutered at younger ages, speak with your veterinarian and ask for their recommendations regarding the right age to spay or neuter your Chiweenie.

a) Effects on Aggression

Intact (non-neutered) males and females are more likely to display aggression related to sexual behavior than are dogs that have been neutered or spayed.

Fighting, particularly in male dogs that is directed at other males, is less common after neutering, and the intensity of other types of aggression, such as irritable aggression in females will be totally eliminated by spaying.

While neutering or spaying is not a treatment for aggression, it can certainly help to minimize the severity and escalation of aggressiveness and is often the first step toward resolving an aggressive behavior problem.

b) What is Neutering?

Neutering is a surgical procedure, carried out by a licensed veterinarian surgeon to render a male dog unable to reproduce.

In males, the surgery is also referred to as *"castration"* because the procedure entails the removal of the young dog's testicles. When the testicles are removed, what is left behind is an empty scrotal sac (which used to contain the puppy's testicles) and this empty sac will soon shrink in size until it is no longer noticeable.

c) Neutering Males

Neutering male Chiweenie puppies before they are six months of age can help to ensure that they will be less likely to suffer from obesity problems when they grow older.

Neutering can also mean that a male Chiweenie will be less likely to have the urge to wander.

Further, waiting until a male Chiweenie is older than six months before having them neutered could mean that they will experience the effects of raging testosterone that will drive them to escape their yards by any means necessary to search out females to mate with.

Non-neutered males also tend to spray or mark territory much more often, both inside and outside the home, and during this time can start to display aggressive tendencies toward other dogs as well as people.

d) What is Spaying?

In female puppies, sterilization, referred to as *"spaying"* is a surgical procedure carried out by a licensed veterinarian, to prevent the female dog from becoming pregnant and to stop regular heat cycles.

The sterilization procedure is much more involved for a female puppy (than for a male), as it requires the removal of both ovaries and the uterus by incision into the puppy's abdominal cavity. The uterus is also removed during this surgery, to prevent the possibility of it becoming infected later on in life.

e) Spaying Females

Preferably, female Chiweenie puppies should be spayed before their very first estrus or heat cycle. Females in heat often appear more agitated and irritable, while sleeping and eating less and some may become extremely aggressive toward other dogs.

Spaying female puppies before their first heat pattern can eliminate these hormonal stressors and reduce the opportunity of mammary glandular tumors. Early spaying also protects against various other potential concerns, such as uterine infections.

f) Effects on General Temperament

Many dog owners often become needlessly worried that a neutered or spayed dog will lose their vigor.

Rest assured that a dog's personality or energy level will not be modified or altered in any way by the neutering process, and in fact, many unfavorable qualities resulting from hormonal impact may resolve after surgery.

Your Chiweenie will certainly not come to be less caring or cheerful, and neither will he or she resent you because you are not denying your dog any essential encounters. You will, however, be acting as a conscientious, informed, and caring Chiweenie guardian.

Further, there is little evidence to suggest that the nature of a female Chiweenie will improve after having a litter of puppies.

What is important is that you do not project your own psychological needs or concerns onto your Chiweenie puppy, because there is no gain to be had from permitting sexual activity in either male or female canines.

For instance, it is not *"abnormal"* or *"mean"* to manage a puppy's reproductive activity by having them sterilized. Rather, it is unkind and irresponsible not to neuter or spay a dog and there are many positive benefits of having this procedure carried out.

g) Effects on Escape and Roaming

A neutered or spayed Chiweenie is less likely to wander. Castrated male dogs have the tendency to patrol smaller sized outdoor areas and are less likely to participate in territorial conflicts with perceived opponents.

NOTE: a Chiweenie that has actually already experienced successful escapes from the yard may continue to wander after they are spayed or neutered.

h) Effects on Problem Elimination

An unsterilized dog may urinate or defecate inside the home or in other undesirable areas in an attempt to stake territorial claims, relieve anxiety, or advertise their available reproductive status.

While neutering or spaying a Chiweenie puppy after they have already begun to inappropriately eliminate or mark territory to announce their sexual availability to other dogs will reduce the more powerful urine odor as well as eliminate the hormonal factors, once this habit has begun, the undesirable behavior may continue to persist after neutering or spaying.

i) Possible Weight Gain

While metabolic changes that occur after spaying or neutering can cause some Chiweenie puppy's to gain weight, often the real culprit for any weight gain is the human who feels guilty for subjecting their puppy to any kind of pain and therefore, they attempt to make themselves feel better by feeding more treats or meals to their Chiweenie companion.

If you are concerned about weight gain after neutering or spaying a Chiweenie puppy, simply adjust their food and treat consumption, as needed, and make sure that they receive adequate daily exercise.

It's a very simply process to change your Chiweenie's food intake according to their physical demands and how they look, and if your Chiweenie puppy's daily exercise and level of activity has not changed after they have been spayed or neutered, there will likely be no change in food management necessary.

3. Why Vaccinate a Puppy?

Puppies need to be vaccinated by a veterinarian in order to provide them with protection against four common and serious diseases.

Vaccination against this common set of diseases is referred to as *"DAPP"*, which stands for **D**istemper, **A**denovirus, **P**arainfluenza and **P**arvo Virus.

Approximate one week after your Chiweenie puppy has completed all three sets of primary DAPP vaccinations they will be fully protected from those specific diseases. Thereafter, most veterinarians will recommend a once a year vaccination for the next year or two.

It has now become common practice to vaccinate adult dogs every three years, and if your veterinarian is insisting on a yearly vaccination for your Chiweenie puppy, you need to ask them why, because to do otherwise is considered by most professionals to be *"over vaccinating"*.

a) Distemper

Canine distemper is a contagious and serious viral illness for which there is currently no known cure.

This deadly virus, which is spread either through the air or by direct or indirect contact with a dog that is already infected, or other distemper carrying wildlife, including ferrets, raccoons, foxes, skunks and wolves, is a relative of the measles virus which affects humans.

Canine distemper is sometimes also called *"hard pad disease"* because some strains of the distemper virus actually cause thickening of the pads on a dog's feet, which can also affect the end of a dog's nose.

In dogs or animals with weak immune systems, death may result two to five weeks after the initial distemper infection.

Early symptoms of distemper include fever, loss of appetite, and mild eye inflammation that may only last a day or two. Symptoms become more serious and noticeable as the disease progresses.

A puppy or dog that survives the distemper virus will usually continue to experience symptoms or signs of the disease throughout their remaining lifespan, including *"hard pad disease"* as well as *"enamel hypoplasia"*, which is damage to the enamel of the puppy's teeth that are not yet formed or that have not yet pushed through the gums.

Enamel hypoplasia is caused when the distemper virus kills the cells that manufacture tooth enamel.

b) Adenovirus

Is a virus that causes infectious canine hepatitis, which can range in severity from very mild to very serious, sometimes resulting in death.

Symptoms can include coughing, loss of appetite, increased thirst and urination, tiredness, runny eyes and nose, vomiting, bruising or bleeding under the skin, swelling of the head, neck and body, fluid accumulation in the abdomen area, jaundice (yellow tinge to the skin), a bluish clouding of the cornea of the eye (called "hepatitis blue eye") and seizures.

There is no specific treatment for infectious canine hepatitis. Treatment of the disease is focused on managing symptoms while the virus runs its course. Hospitalization and intravenous fluid therapy may be required in severe cases.

c) Canine Parainfluenza Virus

The canine parainfluenza virus (CPIV) also referred to as *"canine influenza virus"*, *"greyhound disease"* or *"race flu"*, which is easily spread through the air or by coming into contact with respiratory secretions, was originally a virus that only affected horses.

This disease is believed to have adapted to become contagious to dogs, is easily spread from dog to dog, and may cause symptoms that become fatal.

While the more frequent occurrences of this respiratory infection are seen in areas where there are high dog populations, such as race tracks, boarding kennels and pet stores, this virus is highly contagious to any dog or puppy, at any age.

Symptoms can include a dry, hacking cough, difficulty breathing, wheezing, runny nose and eyes, sneezing, fever, loss of appetite, tiredness, depression and possible pneumonia.

In cases where only a cough exists, tests will be required to determine whether the cause of the cough is the parainfluenza virus or the less serious *"kennel cough"*.

While many dogs can naturally recover from this virus, they will remain contagious, and for this reason, in order to prevent the spread to other animals, aggressive treatment of the virus, with antibiotics and antiviral drugs will be the general course of action.

In more severe cases, a cough suppressant may be prescribed, as well as intravenous fluids to help prevent secondary bacterial infection.

d) Canine Parvovirus

Canine parvovirus (CPV) is a highly contagious viral illness affecting puppies and dogs. Parvovirus also affects other canine species including foxes, coyotes and wolves.

There are two forms of this virus (1) the more common intestinal form, and (2) the less common cardiac form, which can cause death in young puppies.

Symptoms of the intestinal form of parvovirus include vomiting, bloody diarrhea, weight loss, and lack of appetite, while the less common cardiac form attacks the heart muscle.

Early vaccination in young puppies has radically reduced the incidence of canine parvovirus infection, which is easily transmitted either by direct contact with an infected dog, or indirectly, by sniffing an infected dog's feces.

The virus can also be brought into a dog's environment on the bottom of human shoes that may have stepped on infected feces, and there is evidence that this hardy virus can live in ground soil for up to a year.

Recovery from parvovirus requires both aggressive and early treatment. With proper treatment, death rates are relatively low (between 5 and 20%), although chances of survival for puppies are much lower than for older dogs, and in all instances, there is no guarantee of survival.

Treatment of parvovirus requires hospitalization where intravenous fluids and nutrients are administered to help combat dehydration. As well, antibiotics will be given to counteract secondary bacterial infections, and as necessary, medications to control nausea and vomiting may also be given.

Without prompt and proper treatment, dogs that have severe parvovirus infections can die within 48 to 72 hours.

4. Other Diseases and Viruses

a) Rabies Vaccinations

Rabies is a viral disease transmitted by coming into contact with the saliva of an infected animal, usually through a bite.

The virus travels to the brain along the nerves and once symptoms develop, death is almost certainly inevitable, usually following a prolonged period of suffering.

If you plan to travel out of State or across country borders, you will need to make sure that your Chiweenie has an up to date Rabies Vaccination Certificate (NASPHV form 51) indicating they have been inoculated against rabies.
Vaccinating dogs against rabies is also compulsory in most countries in mainland Europe, as is permanent identification and registration of dogs through the use of a Pet Passport.

Those living in a country that is rabies free (UK, Eire) are not required to vaccinate their dogs against rabies, unless they intend to travel.

b) Leishmaniasis

Leishmaniasis is caused by a parasite and is transmitted by a bite from a sand fly.

There is no definitive answer for effectively combating Leishmaniasis, especially since one vaccine will not prevent the known multiple species.

In areas where the known cause is a sand fly, deltamethrin collars (containing a neurotoxic insecticide) worn by the dogs has been proven to be 86% effective.

There are two types of Leishmaniasis: (1) a skin reaction causing hair loss, lesions and ulcerative dermatitis, and (2) a more severe, abdominal organ reaction, which is also known as *"black fever"*. When the disease affects organs of the abdominal cavity the symptoms include:

- loss of appetite
- diarrhea
- severe weight loss
- exercise intolerance
- vomiting
- nose bleed
- tarry feces
- fever
- pain in the joints
- excessive thirst and urination
- inflammation of the muscles

Leishmaniasis spreads throughout the body to most organs, with kidney failure being the most common cause of death. Virtually all infected dogs develop this system wide disease and as much as 90% of those infected will also display skin reactions.

Affected dogs in the US are frequently found to have acquired this infection in another country.

Of note, is that this disease is regularly found in the Middle East, the area around the Mediterranean basin, Portugal, Spain, Africa, South and Central America, southern Mexico and the US, with regular cases reported in Oklahoma and Ohio, where it is found in 20 to 40% of the dog population.

There have also been a few reported cases in Switzerland, northern France and the Netherlands.

NOTE: Leishmaniasis is a *"zoonotic"* infection, which is a contagious disease that can be spread between both animals and humans.

This means that the organisms residing in the Leishmaniasis lesions can be communicated to humans.

Treatment in dogs is often difficult and the dog may suffer from relapses. Leishmaniasis poses a significant risk to the health of your dog, especially if you travel to the Mediterranean.

c) Lyme Disease

This is one of the most common tick-borne diseases in the world, which is transmitted by Borrelia bacteria found in the deer or sheep tick.

Lyme disease, also called *"borreliosis"*, is also a zoonotic disease that can affect both humans and dogs and this disease can be fatal.

The Borrelia bacteria that causes Lyme's disease, is transmitted by slow-feeding, hard-shelled deer or sheep ticks, and the tick usually has to be attached to the dog for a minimum of 18 hours before the infection is transmitted.

Symptoms of this disease in a young or adult dog include:

- recurrent lameness from joint inflammation
- lack of appetite
- depression
- stiff walk with arched back
- sensitivity to touch
- swollen lymph nodes
- fever
- kidney damage
- rare heart or nervous system complications

While Lyme disease has been reported in dogs throughout the United States and Europe, it is most prevalent in the upper Mid-Western states, the Atlantic seaboard, and the Pacific coastal states.

In order to properly diagnose and treat Lyme disease, blood tests will be required, and if the tests are positive, oral antibiotics will be prescribed to treat the conditions.

Prevention is the key to keeping this disease under control because dogs that have had Lyme disease before are still able to get the disease again.

There is a vaccine for Lyme disease and dogs living in areas that have easy access to these ticks should be vaccinated yearly.

d) Rocky Mountain Spotted Fever

This tick-transmitted disease is very often seen in dogs in the East, Midwest, and plains region of the US, and the organisms causing Rocky Mountain Spotted Fever (RMSF) are transmitted by both the American dog tick and the RMSF tick, which must be attached to the dog for a minimum of five hours in order to transmit the disease.

Common symptoms of RMSF include:

- fever
- reduced appetite
- depression
- pain in the joints
- lameness
- vomiting
- diarrhea

Some dogs affected with RMSF may develop heart abnormalities, pneumonia, kidney failure, liver damage, or even neurological signs, such an seizures or unsteady, wobbly or stumbling gait.

Diagnosis of this disease requires blood testing and if the results are positive, oral antibiotics will be given to the infected dog for approximately two weeks.

Dogs that can clear the organism from their systems will recover and after being infected, will remain immune to future infection.

e) Ehrlichiosis

This is another tick borne disease transmitted by both the brown dog tick and the Lone Star Tick.

Ehrlichiosis has been reported in every state in the US, as well as worldwide. Common symptoms include:

- depression
- reduced appetite
- fever
- stiff and painful joints
- bruising

Signs of infection typically occur less than a month after a tick bite and last for approximately four weeks. There is no vaccine available.

Blood tests may be required to test for antibodies and treatment will require a course of antibiotics for up to four weeks in order to completely clear the organism from the infected dog's system.

After a dog has been previously infected, they may develop antibodies to the organism, but will not be immune to being re-infected.

Dogs living in areas of the country where the Ehrlichiosis tick disease are common or widespread may be prescribed low doses of antibiotics during tick season.

f) Anaplasmosis

Deer ticks and western blacklegged ticks are carriers of the bacteria that transmit canine Anaplasmosis.

However, there is also another form of Anaplasmosis (caused by a different bacteria) that is carried by the brown dog tick. Because the deer tick also carries other diseases, some animals may be at risk for developing more than one tick-borne disease at the same time.

Signs of Anaplasmosis are similar to Ehrlichiosis and include painful joints, diarrhea, fever, and vomiting as well as possible nervous system disorders.

A dog will usually begin to show signs of Anaplasmosis within a couple of weeks after infection and diagnosis will require blood and urine testing, and sometimes other specialized laboratory tests.

Treatment is with oral antibiotics for up to 30 days, depending on how severe the infection may be.

When this disease is quickly treated, most dogs will recover completely, however, subsequent immunity is not guaranteed, which means that a dog may be re-infected if exposed again.

g) Tick Paralysis

Tick paralysis is caused when ticks secrete a toxin that affects the nervous system.

Affected dogs show signs of weakness and limpness approximately one week after being first bitten by ticks.

Symptoms usual begin with a change in pitch of the dog's usual bark, which will become softer, and weakness in the rear legs that eventually involves all four legs, which is then followed by the dog showing difficulty breathing and swallowing.

If the condition is not diagnosed and properly treated, death can occur.

Treatment involves locating and removing the tick and then treating the infected dog with tick anti-serum.

h) Canine Coronavirus

While this highly contagious intestinal disease, which is spread through the feces of contaminated dogs, was first discovered in Germany during 1971 when there was an outbreak in sentry dogs, it is now found worldwide.

This virus can be destroyed by most commonly available disinfectants.

Symptoms include:

- diarrhea
- vomiting
- weight loss or anorexia

While deaths resulting from this disease are rare, and treatment generally requires only medication to relieve the diarrhea, dogs that are more severely affected may require intravenous fluids to combat dehydration.

There is a vaccine available, which is usually given to puppies, because they are more susceptible at a young age. This vaccine is also given to show dogs that have a higher risk of exposure to the disease.

i) Leptospirosis

This is a disease that occurs throughout the World that can affect many different kinds of animals, including dogs, and as it is also a zoonotic disease, this means that it can affect humans, too. There is potential for both dogs and humans to die from this disease.

The disease is always present in the environment, which makes it easy for any dog to pick up. This is because it is found in many common animals, such as rats, and wildlife, as well as domestic livestock.

Veterinarians generally see more cases of Leptospirosis in the late summer and fall, which is probably because that is when more pets and wildlife are out and about.

More cases also occur after heavy rainfalls.

The disease is most common in mild or tropical climates around the World, and in the US or Canada, it is more common in states or provinces that receive heavy rainfall.

The good news is that you can protect your dog from leptospirosis by vaccination, and while puppies are not routinely vaccinated against leptospirosis because chances of contracting the disease depends upon the lifestyle of the dog as well as the area in which the dog lives, it makes sense to vaccinate against this disease if you and your dog do live in an area considered a hot spot for leptospirosis, so ask your veterinarian.

City rat populations are a major carrier of leptospirosis.

Cold winter conditions lower the risk because the leptospira organisms do not tolerate the freezing and thawing of near-zero temperatures.

They are killed rapidly by drying, but they persist in standing water, dampness, mud and alkaline conditions.

Most of the infected wild animals and domestic animals that spread leptospirosis do not appear ill.

The leptospira take up residence in the kidneys of infected animals, which can include rats, mice, squirrels, skunks, and raccoons and when these animals void urine, they contaminate their environment with living leptospira.

Dogs usually become infected after sniffing urine or by wading, swimming or drinking contaminated water that has infected urine in it, and this is how the disease passes from animal to animal.

As well, the leptospira can also enter through a bite wound or if a dog eats infected material.

5. Additional Vaccinations

Depending upon where you and your Chiweenie live, your veterinarian may suggest additional vaccinations to help combat diseases that may be more common in your area.

6. When Is a Puppy Vaccinated?

The first vaccination needle is normally given to a puppy around six to eight weeks of age, which means that generally it will be the responsibility of the Chiweenie breeder to ensure that the puppy's first shots have been received before their new owner takes them home.

Thereafter, it will be the new Chiweenie puppy's guardians that will be responsible for ensuring that the next two sets of shots, which are usually given three to four weeks after each other, are given by the new guardian's veterinarian at the proper intervals.

7. De-Worming

De-worming kills internal parasites that your dog or puppy may have.

NOTE: no matter how sanitary your conditions, or where you live, your dog will have internal parasites, because it is not a matter of cleanliness.

It is recommended by the Center for Disease Control (CDC) that puppies be dewormed every 2 weeks until they are 3 months old, and then every month after that, in order to control worms.

Many veterinarians recommend worming dogs for tapeworm and roundworms every 6-12 months.

8. Special Care When Pregnant

As canine pregnancy lasts approximately 63 days, and a Chiweenie female will go into labor within 56 to 66 days after becoming pregnant, a pregnant Chiweenie will require immediate attention when the first signs of pregnancy appear.

Immediately upon noticing signs of pregnancy you will want to take your Chiweenie to your veterinarian to confirm the pregnancy and to receive instructions for the proper feeding and care.

During the first days of pregnancy your Chiweenie may experience morning sickness.

Your veterinarian may recommend increasing food intake or adding an egg or cottage cheese to your Chiweenie's meals and switching to puppy kibble, which is higher in protein, at around the 30 day mark.

As the Chiweenie female becomes heavier with the puppies, she will lose interest in exercising and her other normal activities and will need to sleep more.

When the time for birthing is drawing near, the Chiweenie female will start to display "nesting" characteristics where she will search for a warm and safe place to give birth.

You can help by providing a nesting box and she will likely want to take things into the box to make it more comfortable, such as towels or even a stuffed toy that she will begin to mother.

When the time draws near to whelping, the Chiweenie female may completely lose her appetite and show distress by pacing, panting, and acting uncomfortable.

When the birthing time is near, the dog's temperature needs to be checked, and should be around 100.2 to 100.8 degrees Fahrenheit (37.89 to 38.22 degrees Centigrade).

When her temperature drops to approximately 98 to 99.4 degrees Fahrenheit (36.67 to 37.44 degrees Centigrade), the puppies will usually be born within 24 hours.

If you are at all worried about the birthing process you will want to take the mother Chiweenie immediately to your veterinarian's office.

If all goes well at home, within 5-6 hours of the last puppy's birth, you will need to take the Chiweenie female and her puppies to your veterinarian for a check up to ensure that the female has not retained any puppies or placentas and that the puppies are all in good health.

9. Licensing

Many cities and jurisdictions around the world require that dogs be licensed.

Usually a dog license is an identifying tag that the dog will be required to wear on their collar. The tag will have an identifying number and a contact number for the registering organization, so that if someone finds a lost dog wearing a tag, the owner of the dog can be contacted.

Most dog tags are only valid for one year, and will need to be renewed annually at the beginning of every New Year, which involves paying a fee, which can vary from jurisdiction to jurisdiction.

From one extreme to the next, owners of dogs living in Beijing, China must pay a licensing fee of $600. (£360), while those living in Great Britain require no fee, because licensing of dogs was abolished in 1987.

Ireland and Northern Ireland both require dogs to be licensed and in Germany dog ownership is taxed, rather than requiring licensing, with higher taxes being paid for breeds of dogs deemed to be "dangerous".

Most US states and municipalities have licensing laws in effect and Canadian, Australian and New Zealand dogs also must be licensed, with the yearly fee approximately $30 to $50 (£18 to £30) depending upon whether the dog has been spayed or neutered.

10. Pet Insurance

Pet guardians commonly ask themselves, when considering medical insurance for their dog, whether they can afford not to have it.

On the one hand, in light of all the new treatments and medications that are now available for our dogs, that usually come with a very high price tag, an increasing number of guardians have decided to add pet insurance to their list of monthly expenses.

On the other hand, some humans believe that placing money into a savings account, in case unforeseen medical treatments are required, makes more sense.

Pet insurance coverage can cost anywhere from $2,000 to $6,000 USD (£1201 to £3604) over an average lifespan of a dog, and unless your dog is involved in a serious accident, or contracts a life-threatening disease, you may never need to pay out that much for treatment.

Whether you decide to start a savings account for your Chiweenie so that you will always have funds available for unforeseen health issues, or you decide to buy a health insurance plan, most dog lovers will go to any lengths to save the life of their beloved companions.

Having access to advanced technological tools and procedures means that our dogs are now being offered treatment options that were once only reserved for humans.

Now, some canine conditions that were once considered fatal, are being treated at considerable costs ranging anywhere between $1,000. and $5,000. (£597 and £2,986) and more.

However, even in the face of rapidly increasing costs of caring for our dogs, owners purchasing pet insurance remain a small minority.

In an effort to increase the numbers of people buying pet insurance, insurers have teamed with the American Kennel Club and Petco Animal Supplies to offer the insurance, and more than 1,600 companies, such as Office Depot and Google, offer pet insurance coverage to their employees as an optional employee benefit.

Even though you might believe that pet insurance will be your savior anytime your dog needs a trip to the vet's office, you really need to be careful when considering an insurance plan, because there are many policies that contain small print excluding certain ages, hereditary or chronic conditions.

Unfortunately, most people don't consider pet insurance when their pets are healthy because buying pet insurance means playing the odds, and unless your dog becomes seriously ill, you end up paying for something that may never happen.

However, just like automobile insurance, you can't buy it after you've had that accident.

Therefore, since many of us, in today's uncertain economy, may be hard pressed to pay a high veterinarian bill, generally speaking, the alternative of paying monthly pet insurance premiums will provide peace of mind and improved veterinarian care for our best friends.

Shop around, because as with all insurance policies, pet insurance policies will vary greatly between companies and the only way to know for certain exactly what sort of coverage you are buying is to be holding a copy of that policy in your hand so that you can clearly read what will and what will not be covered.

Don't forget to carefully read the fine print to avoid any nasty surprises, because the time to discover that a certain procedure will not be covered is not when you are in the middle of filing a claim.

Before Purchasing a Policy

There are several considerations to be aware of before choosing to purchase a pet insurance policy, including:

- Is your dog required to undergo a physical exam?
- Is there a waiting period before the policy becomes active?
- What percentage of the bill does the insurance company pay — after the deductible?
- Are payments limited or capped in any way?
- Are there co-pays (cost to you up front)?
- Does the plan cover pre-existing conditions?
- Does the plan cover chronic or recurring medical problems?
- Can you choose any vet or animal hospital to treat your pet?
- Are prescription medications covered?
- Are you covered when traveling with your pet?
- Does the policy pay if your pet is being treated and then dies?

When you love your dog and worry that you may not have the funds to cover an emergency medical situation that could unexpectedly cost thousands, the right pet insurance policy will provide both peace of mind and better health care for your beloved fur friend.

11. Identifying and Finding Lost Dogs

a) Micro-Chipping

A microchip implant is a tiny integrated circuit, approximately twice the size of a large grain of rice, enclosed in glass that is implanted under the skin of a dog (or other animal) with a syringe.

The chip uses passive Radio Frequency Identification (RFID) technology, and is also known as a PIT tag (Passive Integrated Transponder).

The microchip is usually implanted, without anesthetic, into the scruff of a dog's neck by a veterinarian or shelter.

The microchip has no internal power source, which means that they must be read by a scanner or *"interrogator"* which energizes the capacitor in the chip, which then sends radio signals back to the scanner so that the identifying number can be read.

Manufacturers of microchips often donate scanners to animal shelters and veterinarian clinics and hospitals.

While many communities are proposing making micro-chipping of all dogs mandatory, such as N. Ireland, and micro-chipping is a requirements for any dogs traveling to the state of Hawaii, many others are not especially pleased with this idea because they believe it's just more big business for little reward.

For instance, while approximately one quarter of European dogs have a microchip implant, the idea is definitely lacking in popularity in the United States, where only 5% of dogs are micro-chipped.

Even though micro-chipping is used by animal shelters, pounds, animal control officers, breeders and veterinarians, in order to help return a higher percentage of lost canines to their owners, some of the resistance to this idea can be explained by inherent problems with the ability of some organizations to correctly read the implants.

As an example, if the scanner is not tuned to the same frequency as the implanted microchip, it will not be read, which renders the process useless.

Pet microchips are manufactured with different frequencies, including 125 kHz, 128 kHz and 134.2 kHz.

While approximately 98% of the pet microchips in the US use 125 kHz, those in Europe use 134.2 kHz.

In other words, if the facility reading your dog's microchip does not have a compatible scanner, your dog will not be identified and returned to you.

Further, what may turn out to be worse than the scanner incompatibility problem could be increasing evidence to indicate that microchips might cause cancer.

As well some microchips will migrate inside the dog's body and while they may start out in the dogs neck, they could end up in their leg or some other body part.

You will have to weigh information known about microchips, including possible cancer risks, and the odds of losing your dog against whether or not a microchip is something you want to have for your Chiweenie.

Whether or not you choose a microchip for your dog, generally the cost ranges between $25 and $50 (£15 and £30) depending on what your veterinarian may charge for this service.

b) Tattooing

Dogs are tattooed to help identify them in case they are lost or stolen and many dog guardians prefer this safe, simple solution over micro-chipping.

Tattooing does not require locating a scanner that reads the correct frequency and there are no known side effects.

Because a tattoo is visible, it is immediately recognizable and reported when a lost dog is found, which means that tattooing could easily be the most effective means of identification available.

As well, dog thieves are less likely to steal a dog that has a permanent visible form of identification. There are several registries for tattooed dogs, including the National Dog Tattoo Registry in the UK, which has a network of Accredited Tattooists across the UK.

The fee for tattooing and registering a dog for their lifetime is approximately £25.

In the United States, the National Dog Registry (NDR) was founded in 1966 and since then, NDR has supervised, directed, conducted, or overseen the tattooing of more than 6 million animals.

The cost for tattooing a single dog is approximately $10. plus a one-time registration fee of $45.

c) Where to Look

If your Chiweenie goes missing, there are many places you can contact and steps you can take that may help you locate your lost dog, including:

- retracing your dog's last known location;

- contacting your friends and neighbours;

- putting up flyers on telephone poles throughout your neighbourhood, with your contact details and a photograph of your dog;

- calling all local shelters and pounds every day;

- contacting local rescue organisations;

- contacting your breeder;

• contacting local schools -- children might have seen your dog in their neighbourhood;

• distributing flyers with a photograph of your dog and your contact details in all neighbourhood stores and businesses;

• contacting all businesses that deal with lost pets;

• posting a picture on your Facebook or other social media;

• asking your local radio station for help;

• advertising in your local newspaper.

12. Yearly Cost of Ownership

It can be difficult to accurately estimate what the cost of owning every Chiweenie might be because there are too many variables and unexpected medical problems, which might arise that may not otherwise be considered average.

For instance, you may like to buy fancy clothes, new collars and leashes every year, the latest toys and gadgets, or the most expensive food for your dog every week that might also not be considered average.

However, when thinking about sharing your life with a dog, it's important to consider more than just the daily cost of feeding your Chiweenie.

Many humans do not think about whether or not they can truly afford to care for a dog before they bring one home, and not being prepared can cause stress and problems later on.

Remember that being financially responsible for your Chiweenie is a large part of being a good guardian.

Beyond the initial investment of purchasing your Chiweenie puppy from a reputable breeder, for most guardians, owning a

Chiweenie will include the costs associated with the following:

- food
- treats
- pee pads, poop bags, potty patches
- leashes and collars
- safety harnesses
- travel kennels or bags
- house training pens
- clothing
- toys
- beds
- professional grooming or equipment
- shampoo and conditioner
- neutering or spaying
- regular veterinary care
- obedience or dog whispering classes
- pet sitting, walking or boarding
- pet insurance
- tattooing
- micro-chipping
- yearly licensing
- unexpected emergencies

As you can see from the list above, there are many variables involved with being a canine guardian that may or may not apply to your particular situation.

For instance, depending upon where you shop, what type of food and how much you feed your Chiweenie, what sort of veterinarian or grooming care you choose, whether or not you have pet insurance and what types of items you purchase for your Chiweenie's well being, the yearly cost of owning a Chiweenie could be estimated at anywhere between $700 and $3,000 (£420 and £1,800) per year.

Other contributing factors that may have an effect on the overall yearly cost of owning a Chiweenie can include the region where you live, the weather, the accessibility of the items you need, your own lifestyle preferences and your Chiweenie's age and individual needs.

NOTE: the more popular a particular breed may be, and the more positive traits a particular breed may enjoy will also make the cost of initially purchasing a puppy from a breeder more costly.

Chapter 12: Coat Colors and Types

The Chiweenie will tend toward having a short, smoother haired coat, unless one of the parents is a longer or curly coated Dachshund.

The ears of a Chiweenie can be either erect, like the Chihuahua, or floppy, like the Dachshund.

Coat colors come in a wide variety, depending on the coat color of the parents and which parent's genes are more dominant.

When choosing a Chiweenie as your companion, there are so many coat color combinations possible, that even the most discerning human will be able to find the perfect match.

For instance, solid colors include apricot, black, chocolate, gold, grey, red, tan, silver or white while they also may frequently have a mix of two or more colors in one coat, such as black, white and brown, black and dark brown with tan markings, or a lighter brown or tan with black points.

Interestingly, it is not uncommon for each puppy in a single litter to display a variety of colors and for each of the puppies to look entirely different in coloring from one another.

The coat on the Chiweenie will generally be very low maintenance, requiring a brushing with a soft bristle brush at least once a week and a bath once a month.

This will be a shedding dog and as such may not be appropriate for those humans suffering from allergies.

1. Puppy Coats

By the time the Chiweenie puppy is approximately five or six months old, they will have grown in their adult coat, and if one of the parents had a short or long coat, some of the puppies may also have longer coats.

The coat of the Chiweenie is known for its soft, Dachshund-like texture, although if crossed with a long-haired Chihuahua, some of these dogs will look more like a longer haired Chihuahua, with a longer silkier, or wavy coat.

The Chiweenie hybrid coat can be a variety of colors including all the colors of a Chihuahua and may also display tan or black points.

2. Adult Coats

The Chiweenie adult coat will begin to grow in at approximately 9-months of age. The entire process and complete change over to the adult coat will usually take 9 or 10 months or longer to fully complete.

During this time of coat change over, it will be very important to thoroughly brush your young dog's coat every day to help remove dead hair while the new coat grows in. The Chiweenie will require minimal brushing to keep them looking their best.

3. Coat Types

The Chiweenie may take on more characteristics of the Dachshund coat or more of the Chihuahua coat, or their coat may be any combination of the two.

a) More Dachshund

If the Chiweenie tends more to the traditional Dachshund type of short coat, they will have a flat coat that will be low shedding. If one of the parents is a longer haired Dachshund the coat of the puppy may be silky and of medium length.

b) More Chihuahua

If the Chiweenie tends more to the shorter coated Chihuahua, they will have hair that is straight and silky and a coat that will shed moderately. If the Chihuahua parent has a longer coat, the puppies may also have longer coats.

4. Defining Features

The most distinctive features of the Chiweenie is their large expressive eyes, and in some puppies, also their large, erect ears.

As well, many hybrid Chiweenie dogs take on the longer, low body of the Dachshund parent.

Chapter 13: Grooming

You will want to get your Chiweenie puppy used to the routine of grooming early on, so that they will not be traumatized for the rest of their life, every time grooming is necessary.

Not taking the time to regularly involve your Chiweenie puppy in grooming sessions could lead to serious, unwanted behavior that may include trauma to your dog, not to mention stress or injury to yourself in the form of biting and scratching, that could result in a lifetime of unhappy grooming sessions.

When you neglect regular, daily or at least a weekly at home grooming session with your puppy or dog to remove dead hair and check toenails, this will not only cost you and your canine companion, in terms of possible trauma it may also cost you in veterinarian fees should you not be aware of a problem that could have been discovered early on during regular grooming sessions.

An effective home regimen will depend on the length of your Chiweenie's coat, and should include not just surface brushing, but also getting to all those sensitive areas easily missed around the ears and collar area, the armpit area, and the back end and tail.

Do not allow yourself to get caught in the *"my dog doesn't like it"* trap which is an excuse many owners will use to avoid regular grooming sessions.

When you allow your dog to dictate whether they will permit a grooming session, you are setting a dangerous precedent that could lead to lifetime of trauma for both you and your Chiweenie.

When humans neglect daily grooming routines, many dogs develop a heightened sensitivity, especially with regard to having their legs and feet held, their ears inspected, or their nails clipped touched, and will do anything they can to avoid the process when you need to groom them.

Make a pact with yourself right from the first day you bring your Chiweenie puppy home, never to neglect a regular grooming routine and not to avoid sensitive areas, such as trimming toenails or brushing teeth, just because your dog may not particular *"like"* it.

Remember that a few minutes of regular grooming sessions each day with your Chiweenie is also wonderful opportunity for closely bonding.

1. Bath Time

Step One: before you get your Chiweenie anywhere near the water, it's important to make sure that you brush out any debris, or dead hair from their coat before you begin the bathing process.

As well, removing any debris from your dog's coat beforehand will make the entire process easier on both you, your dog, and your drains, which will become clogged with dead hair if you don't remove it beforehand.

Step Two: if your Chiweenie has a longer coat, the process will be much easier if you first spray the coat with a light mist of leave-in conditioner before brushing. This will also help to protect the hair strands against breakage.

Step Three: whether you're bathing your Chiweenie in your laundry tub, bathtub or sink, you will always want to first lay down a rubber bath mat to provide a more secure footing for your dog and to prevent your tub or sink from being scratched.

Step Four: have everything you need for the bath (shampoo, conditioner, sponge, towels) right next to the sink or tub, so you don't have to go searching once your dog is already in the water.

TIP: place cotton balls in your Chiweenie's ear canals to prevent accidental splashes from entering the ear canal that could later cause an ear infection.

Step Five: fill the tub or sink with four to six inches of lukewarm water (not too hot as dogs are more sensitive to hot water than us humans) and put your Chiweenie in the water. Completely wet your dog's coat right down to the skin by using a detachable showerhead. If you don't have a spray attachment, a cup or pitcher will work just as well.

TIP: no dog likes to have water poured over their head and into their eyes, so use a wet sponge or wash cloth to wet the head area.

Step Six: apply shampoo as indicated on the bottle instructions by beginning at the head and working your way down the back. Be careful not to get shampoo in the eyes, nose, mouth or ears. Comb the shampoo lather through your dog's hair with your fingers, making sure you don't miss the areas under the legs and tail.

Step Seven: after allowing the shampoo to remain in your dog's coat for a couple of minutes, thoroughly rinse the Chiweenie's coat, right down to the skin with clean, lukewarm water using the spray attachment, cup or pitcher. Comb through your dog's coat with your fingers to make sure all shampoo residue has been completely rinsed away.

TIP: any shampoo remaining in a dog's coat will lead to irritation and itching. Once you've rinsed, take the time to rinse again, especially in the armpits and underneath the tail area.

Use your hands to gently squeeze all excess water from your dog's coat.

Step Eight: apply conditioner as indicated on the bottle instructions and work the conditioner throughout your Chiweenie's coat. Leave the conditioner in your dog's coat for two minutes and then thoroughly rinse again with warm water, unless the conditioner you are using is a *"leave-in"*, no-rinse formula.

NOTE: The best conditioner for a Chiweenie will contain mink oil, which adds a gloss to deepen and enrich the natural color of the coat.

It is also a good idea to choose a brand of conditioner that contains sunscreen to help protect from ultraviolet radiation when your dog is outside on sunny days.

Applying a good conditioner containing protein to your Chiweenie's coat after bathing will help to rebuild, restructure and protect the coat by bonding to the shaft of each individual hair.

Pull the plug on your sink or tub and let the water drain away as you use your hands to squeeze excess water from your Chiweenie's legs and feet.

Step Nine: immediately out of the water, wrap your Chiweenie in dry towels so they don't get cold and use the towels to gently squeeze out extra water before you allow them to shake and spray water everywhere.

If your dog has longer hair, do not rub their coat with the towels, as this will create tangles and breakage in the longer hair.

Dry your Chiweenie right away with your hand held hairdryer and be careful not to let the hot air get too close to their skin.

TIP: if your Chiweenie's hair is longer, blow the hair in the direction of growth to help prevent breakage and if the hair is short, you can use your hand or a soft brush or comb to lift and fluff the coat to help it dry more quickly.

TIP: place your hand between the hairdryer and your Chiweenie's hair so that they will never get a direct blast of hot air and never blow air directly into their face or ears.

Don't forget to remove the cotton balls from their ears.

2. Ear Care

There are many ear cleaning creams, drops, oils, rinses, solutions and wipes formulated for cleaning your dog's ears that you can purchase from your local pet store or veterinarian's office.

Or you may prefer to use a home remedy that will just as efficiently clean your Chiweenie's ears, such as Witch Hazel or a 50:50 mixture of hydrogen peroxide and purified water.

TIP: if you are going to make your own ear cleaning solution, find a bottle with a nozzle, measure your solution, properly diluted and mixed into the bottle, and use your preparation to saturate a cotton makeup remove pad to wipe out the visible part of your dog's ears. Always make sure the ears are totally dried after cleaning.

3. Eye Care

Every dog should have their eyes regularly wiped with a warm, damp cloth to remove build up of daily secretions in the corners of the eyes that can be unattractive and uncomfortable for the dog as the hair becomes glued together.

If this build up is not removed every day, it can quickly become a cause of bacterial yeast growth that can lead to eye infections.

When you take a moment every day to gently wipe your dog's eyes with a warm, moist cloth, you will help to keep your dog's eyes comfortable and infection free.

4. Nail Care

Allowing your Chiweenie to have long, untrimmed nails can result in various health hazards including infections or an irregular and uncomfortable gait that can result in damage to their skeleton.

Although most dogs do not particular enjoy the process of having their nails trimmed, and most humans find the exercise to be a little scary, regular nail trimming is a very important grooming practice that should never be overlooked.

In order to keep your adult Chiweenie's toenails in good condition and the proper length, you will need to purchase a plier type nail trimmer at a pet store and learn how to correctly use it.

NOTE: when your Chiweenie is a small puppy, it will be best to trim their nails with a pair of nail scissors, which you can purchase at any pet store, that are smaller and easier to use on puppy nails. All you need to do is snip off the curved tip of each nail.

Further, if you want your dog's nails to be smooth, without the sharp edges clipping alone can create, you will also want to invest in a toenail file or a special, slow speed, rotary Dremel™ trimmer, equipped with a sanding disk, which is designed especially for dog nails. Some dogs will prefer the rotary trimmer to the squeezing sensation of the nail clipper and when you keep your dog's nails regularly trimmed, the Dremel™ may be the only tool you will ever need.

NOTE: <u>never</u> use a regular Dremel™ tool on a dog's toenails as it will be too high speed and will burn your dog's toenails. Only use a slow speed Dremel™, Model 7300-PT Pet Nail Grooming Tool.

5. Dental Care

As a conscientious Chiweenie guardian you will need to regularly care for your dog's teeth throughout their entire life.

a) Retained Primary Teeth

Often times a young dog will not naturally lose their puppy or baby teeth, especially those with small jaws, like the Chiweenie, without intervention from a licensed veterinarian.

Therefore, keep a close watch on your puppy's teeth around the age of 6 or 7 months of age to make certain that the baby teeth have fallen out and that the adult teeth have space to grown in.

If your Chiweenie puppy has not naturally lost all their baby teeth, any remaining teeth will need to be pulled, in order to allow room for the adult teeth to properly grow in, and the best time to do this will be at the same time they visit the veterinarian's office to be spayed or neutered.

Smaller dogs, like the Chiweenie, have a smaller jaw, which can result in more problems with teeth overcrowding.

An overcrowded mouth can cause teeth to grow unevenly or crooked and food and plaque to more easily build up, which will eventually result in bacterial grow on the surface of the teeth, causing bad breath, gum and dental disease.

b) Periodontal Disease

Please be aware that 80% of three-year-old dogs suffer from periodontal disease and bad breath because their guardians do <u>not</u> look after their dog's teeth.

What makes this shocking statistic even worse is that it is entirely possible to prevent canine gum disease and bad breath.

The pain associated with periodontal disease will make your dog's life miserable, as it will be painful for them to eat and the associated bacteria can infect many parts of the dog's body, including the heart, kidney, liver and brain, all of which they will have to suffer in silence.

If your Chiweenie has bad breath, this could be the first sign of gum disease caused by plaque build-up on the teeth.

As well, if your Chiweenie is drooling excessively, this may be a symptom secondary to dental disease. Your dog may be experiencing pain or the salivary glands may be reacting to inflammation from excessive bacteria in the mouth.

If you notice your Chiweenie drooling, you will want to have them professionally examined at your veterinarian's office.

c) Teeth Brushing

Slowly introduce your Chiweenie to teeth brushing early on in their young life so that they will not fear it.

Begin with a finger cap toothbrush when they are young puppies, and then move to a soft bristled toothbrush, or even an electric brush, as all you have to do is hold it against the teeth while the brush does all the work. Sometimes with a manual brush, you may brush too hard and cause the gums to bleed.

Never use human toothpaste or mouthwash on your dog's teeth because dogs cannot spit and human toothpaste that contains toxic fluoride will be swallowed. There are many flavored dog toothpastes available at the pet store or veterinarian's office.

Also, it's a good idea to get your dog used to the idea of occasionally having their teeth scraped or scaled, especially the back molars which tend to build up plaque. Be very careful if you are doing this yourself because the tools are sharp.

TIP: if you need help keeping your dog's mouth open while you do a quick brush or scrape, get yourself a piece of hard material (rubber or leather) that they can bite down on, so that they cannot fully close their mouth while you work on their teeth.

When your Chiweenie is a young puppy, take the time to get them used to having their mouth handled and your fingers rubbing their teeth and gums.

Next, buy some canine toothpaste at your local pet store specially flavored to appeal to dogs and apply this to your dog's teeth with your finger.

Then slowly introduce the manual or electric toothbrush to your Chiweenie. When you go slowly, they will get used to the buzzing and vibrating of the electric brush, which will do a superior job of cleaning their teeth.

First, let them see the electric brush, then let them hear it buzzing, and before you put it in their mouth, let them feel the buzzing sensation on their body, while you move it slowly toward their head and muzzle.

When your Chiweenie will allow you to touch their muzzle while the brush is turned on, the next step is to brush a couple of teeth at a time until they get used to having them all brushed at the same time.

Always happily praise them for allowing you to brush their teeth, especially when they are first getting used to the idea.

Whether you let the electric toothbrush do the work for you, or you are using a manual toothbrush, make certain that you brush in a circular motion with the bristles of the brush angled so that they get underneath the gum line to help prevent plaque buildup, gum disease and loose teeth.

d) Teeth Scaling

Use of a tooth scraper or scaling tool once or twice a month can help to remove plaque buildup. Most accumulation will be found on the outside of the teeth and on the back molars, near the gum line.

Go slowly and carefully because these tools are sharp and only do this when your dog is calm and relaxed, a little bit at a time.

e) Healthy Teeth Tips

Despite what most dog owners might put up with as normal, it is not normal for your dog to have smelly dog breath or canine halitosis. Bad breath is the first sign of an unhealthy mouth, which could involve gum disease or tooth decay.

The following tips will help keep your Chiweenie's mouth and teeth healthy:

- keep your dog's teeth sparkling white and their breath fresh by using old-fashioned hydrogen peroxide as your doggy toothpaste. Hydrogen peroxide is what's in the human whitening toothpaste. There will be such a small amount on the brush that it will not harm your dog, and will kill any bacteria in your dog's mouth.

- many canine toothpastes are formulated with active enzymes to help keep tartar build-up at bay.

- help prevent tooth plaque and doggy halitosis by feeding your dog natural, hard bones at least once a month, which will also help to remove tartar while polishing and keeping their teeth white.

- Feed large bones so there is no danger of swallowing, and do NOT boil the bones first because this makes the bone soft (which defeats the purpose of removing plaque), and boiling could cause bones to splinter into smaller pieces that could create a choking or puncturing hazard for your dog.

- smaller dogs, such as the Chiweenie tend to be more vulnerable to teeth and gum problems, therefore, you really need to be brushing their teeth every single day.

- feed a daily dental chew or hard biscuit to help to remove tartar while exercising jaws and massaging gums. Some dental chews contain natural breath freshening cinnamon, cloves or chlorophyll.

- coconut oil also helps to prevent smelly dog breath while giving your dog's digestive, immune and metabolic functions a boost at the same time. Dogs love the taste, so add ¼ teaspoon to your Chiweenie's dinner and their breath will soon be much sweeter.

Keep your Chiweenie's mouth comfortable and healthy by getting into the habit of brushing their teeth every night before bedtime.

6. Skin Care

Keeping your Chiweenie's coat clean by regularly bathing with canine shampoo and conditioner and free from debris and parasites, as well as providing plenty of clean water and feeding them a high quality diet free from allergy-causing ingredients will go a long way toward keeping their skin healthy and itch-free and their coat shiny and healthy looking.

7. Brushing and Combing

An often over looked task, that is a necessary part of maintaining the health of a Chiweenie, is daily brushing and combing.

As well, taking time to brush and comb your Chiweenie's coat will also give you an opportunity to bond with your dog, while identifying any problems (such as lumps or bumps and matted hair) early on, before they may become more serious.

Make sure that your grooming sessions are as pleasant as possible by choosing the right tools for a Chiweenie and their type and length of coat.

You will need minimal brushes and combs to keep your Chiweenie's coat in good condition, including a slicker brush for longer haired dogs, and a bristle brush for smooth coated dogs.

As well as one or two brushes, you will need to invest in a flea comb.

8. Equipment & Supplies Required

A **slicker brush** has short, thin, wire bristles arranged closely together and anchored to a flat, often rectangular, surface that's attached to a handle.

A slicker brush is an ideal grooming tool for helping to remove mats and tangles from a Chiweenie who has a longer coat. Slicker brushes are often used as a finishing brush after brushing with the bristle brush to smooth the dog's coat and create a shiny finish.

A **bristle brush** can be used to help remove debris and dead hair from the coat and also to help distribute natural oils to keep the coat looking healthy and shiny.

A **metal comb** can also be used for grooming longer haired Chiweenies. Most metal combs have a combination of widely spaced and narrow spaced teeth and are designed so that if you run into a tangle, you can switch to the wider spaced teeth while you work it out, without pulling and irritating your dog.

NOTE: Some combs have rotating teeth which makes the process of removing tangles from your Chiweenie's coat much easier on them without the pain of pulling and snagging.

Flea combs, as the name suggests, are designed for the specific purpose of removing fleas from a dog's coat.

A flea comb is usually small in size for maneuvering in tight spaces, and may be made of plastic or metal with the teeth of the comb placed very close together to trap hiding fleas.

Nail clippers or scissors (and/or a slow speed pet Dremel) will be tools you need to use every couple of weeks or more, depending on how quickly your dog's nails grow and what types of surfaces they may be walking on.

9. Products

a) Shampoos

NEVER make the mistake of using human shampoo or conditioner for bathing your Chiweenie because dogs have a different pH balance than humans.

For example, shampoo for humans has a pH balance of 5.5, whereas shampoo formulated for our canine companions has an almost neutral pH balance of 7.5.

Any shampoo with a lower pH balance will be harmful to your dog because it will be too harshly acidic for their coat and skin, which can create skin problems.

Always purchase a shampoo for your dog that is specially formulated to be gentle and moisturizing on your Chiweenie's coat and skin, that will not strip the natural oils, and which will nourish your dog's coat to give it a healthy shine.

As a general rule, always read the instructions provided on the shampoo bottle, and avoid shampoos containing insecticides or harsh chemicals.

TIP: if your Chiweenie is suffering from an infestation of fleas, you may want to bathe them with shampoo containing pyrethrum (a botanical extract found in small, white daisies) or a shampoo containing citrus or tea tree oil.

b) Conditioners

While many of us humans use a conditioner after we shampoo our own hair, a large number of canine guardians forget to use a conditioner on our own dog's coat after bathing.

Even if the bathing process is one that you wish to complete as quickly as possible, you will want to reconsider this little oversight because, just as conditioning our human hair improves its condition, the same is true for our dog's coat.

Conditioning your Chiweenie's coat will not only make it look and feel better, conditioning will also add additional benefits, including:

- preventing the escape of natural oils and moisture;
- keeping the coat cleaner for a longer period of time;
- repairing a coat that has become damaged or dry;
- restoring a soft, silky feel;
- helping the coat dry more quickly;
- protection from the heat of the dryer and breakage of longer coats during toweling, combing or brushing;

Spend the extra two minutes to condition your Chiweenie's coat after bathing because the benefits of doing so will be appreciated by both you and your dog that will have an overall healthy coat and skin with a natural shine.

c) De-tanglers

There are many de-tangling products you can purchase which will make the job of combing a longer coat much easier on both you and your Chiweenie.

De-tangling products work by making the hair slippery, and while some de-tanglers work well when used full strength, you may prefer a lighter, spray-in product.

As well, there are silicone products and grooming powders, or you can even use cornstarch to effectively lubricate the hair to help with removing mats and tangles before bathing.

d) Styptic Powder

You will always want to avoid causing any pain when trimming your Chiweenie's toenails, because you don't want to destroy their trust in you regularly performing this necessary task.

However, accidents do happen, therefore if you accidentally cut into the vein in the toenail, know that you will cause your dog pain, and that the toenail will bleed.

Therefore, it is always a good idea to keep some styptic powder (often called "Kwik Stop") in your grooming kit. Dip a moistened finger into the powder and apply it immediately to the end of the bleeding nail.

The quickest way to stop a nail from bleeding is to immediately apply styptic powder and firm pressure for a few seconds.

TIP: if you do not have styptic powder available, there are several home remedies that can help stop the bleeding, including a mixture of baking soda and cornstarch, or simply cornstarch alone. Also, a cold, wet teabag or rubbing with scent-free soap can also be effective. These home remedies will not be as instantly effective as styptic powder.

e) Ear Powders

Ear powders, which can be purchased at any pet store, are designed to help keep your dog's ears dry while at the same time inhibiting the growth of bacteria that can lead to infections.

f) Ear Cleaning Solutions

Your local pet store will offer a wide variety of ear cleaning creams, drops, oils, rinses or wipes specially formulated for cleaning your dog's ears.

As well, there are also many home remedies that will just as efficiently clean your dog's ears.

NOTE: because a dog's ears are a very sensitive area, always read the labels before purchasing products and avoid any solutions that list alcohol as the main ingredient.

g) Home Ear Cleaning Solutions

The following are three effective home solutions that will efficiently clean your dog's ears:

Witch Hazel is a natural anti-inflammatory that works well to cleanse and protect against infection while encouraging faster healing of minor skin traumas.

A 50:50 solution of **Organic Apple Cider Vinegar and Purified Water** has been used as an external folk medicine for decades. This mixture is a gentle and effective solution that kills germs while naturally healing.

A 50:50 solution of **Hydrogen Peroxide and Purified Water** is useful for cleansing wounds and dissolving earwax.

Whatever product you decide to use for cleaning your dog's ears, always be careful about what you put into your dog's ears and thoroughly dry them after cleaning.

h) Canine Toothpastes

When it comes time to brush a dog's teeth, this is where many guardians fail miserably, often using the excuse that *"my dog doesn't like it"*.

Whether they like it or otherwise, is not the issue, because in order to keep your Chiweenie healthy, they must have healthy teeth and the only way to ensure this, is to brush their teeth every day.

The many canine toothpastes on the market are usually flavored with beef or chicken in an attempt to appeal to the dog's taste buds, while others may be infused with mint or some other breath freshening ingredient in an attempt to appeal to humans by improving the dog's breath.

Honestly, your dog is not going to be begging for you to brush his or her teeth no matter how tasty the paste might be, therefore, effectiveness, in the shortest period of time, will be more of a deciding factor than whether or not your dog prefers the taste of the toothpaste.

Some dog toothpastes contain baking soda, which is the same mild abrasive found in many human pastes, and is designed to gently scrub the teeth. However, just how much time you will have to spend scrubbing your dog's teeth, before they've had enough, may be too minimal to make these pastes very effective.

Other types of canine toothpastes are formulated with enzymes that are designed to work chemically by breaking down tartar or plaque in the dog's mouth. These pastes do not need to be washed off your dog's teeth and are safe for them to swallow. Whether or not they remain on the dog's teeth long enough to do any good might be debatable.

TIP: old-fashioned hydrogen peroxide cleans while killing germs and keeping teeth white. Just dip your dog's toothbrush in a capful of hydrogen peroxide, shake off the excess, and brush their teeth. There will be such a small amount in your dog's mouth that you don't need to worry about them swallowing it.

i) Paw Creams

Depending upon the types of surfaces our canine counterparts usually walk on, they may suffer from cracked or rough pads. You can restore resiliency and keep your Chiweenie's paws in healthy condition by regularly applying a cream or lotion to protect their paw pads.

TIP: a good time to do this is just after you have clipped their nails.

NOTE: if you live in a hot climate, be aware that sidewalks and road surfaces can get extremely hot for your dog's feet. As well, a small dog, such as the Chiweenie is that much closer to the hot road or sidewalk surface, which means that on a hot day, they will be getting doubly heated from both sides. If it's hot out, walk them on grassy areas only, or carry them.

Chapter 14: Socializing

Most Chiweenies are naturally friendly and social dogs, however, they will still need to be exposed to different people, places and unusual sights and sounds when they are puppies.

Any dog that is not regularly socialized may become shy or suspicious of unfamiliar or unusual people or circumstances, which could lead to nervous or fearful behavior.

1. With Other Dogs and Pets

Generally speaking, the majority of an adult dog's habits and behavioral traits will be formed between the ages of birth and one year of age.

This is why it will be very important to introduce your Chiweenie puppy to a wide variety of locations, sights, sounds, smells and situations during this formative period in their young life.

Your Chiweenie puppy will learn how to behave, in all these various circumstances, by following your lead, feeling your energy and watching how you react in every situation.

For instance, never accidentally reward your Chiweenie puppy or dog for displaying nervousness, fear or growling at another dog or person by picking them up.

Picking up a Chiweenie puppy or dog at this time, when they are displaying unbalanced energy, actually turns out to be a reward for them, and you will be teaching them to continue with this type of behavior.

As well, picking up a puppy literally places them in a top dog position, where they have the higher ground and literally become more dominant than the person or dog they may have just growled at.

The correct action to take in such a situation is to gently correct your Chiweenie puppy, with a firm, yet calm energy by distracting them with a "no", or a quick sideways snap of the leash to get their attention back on you, so that they learn to let you deal with the situation on their behalf.

If you allow a fearful, nervous or shy puppy deal with situations that unnerve them without your direction, they may learn to react with fear or aggression to unfamiliar circumstances and you will have created a problem that could escalate into something quite serious as they grow older.

The same is true of situations where a young puppy may feel the need to protect itself from a larger or older dog that may come charging in for a sniff.

It is the guardian's responsibility to protect the puppy so that they do not feel that they must react with fear or aggression in order to protect themselves.

Once your Chiweenie puppy has received all their vaccinations, you can take them out to public dog parks and various locations where many dogs and people are found.

Before allowing them to interact with other dogs or puppies, take them for a disciplined walk on leash so that they will be a little tired and less likely to immediately pounce excitedly on all other dogs.

Keep your puppy on leash and close beside you, because most young puppies are a bundle of out of control energy, and you need to protect them while teaching them how far they can go before they may get themselves into trouble with adult dogs that might not appreciate their excited playfulness.

Remember that they may not have experienced the company of other dogs since you brought them home, and now that they have completed their course of vaccinations, they will understandably be excited and perhaps a little hesitant about seeing dogs again.

Keep a close watch on your Chiweenie puppy to make sure they are not being overwhelmed by too many other dogs, or getting overly excited and stressed or nervous, because it is your job to protect your puppy.

If your puppy shows any signs of aggression or domination toward another puppy, dog or person, you must immediately step in and calmly discipline them, otherwise by doing nothing, you will be allowing them to get into situations that could become serious behavioral issues as they grow in age and size.

No matter the age or size of your Chiweenie puppy, allowing them to display aggression or domination over another dog or person is never a laughing matter and this type of behavior must be immediately curtailed.

2. With Other People

Take your puppy everywhere with you and introduce them to many different people of all ages, sizes and ethnicities.

This will be easy to do, because most people will automatically be drawn to you when they see you have a puppy because few humans can resist a puppy, especially one as cute as a Chiweenie.

Most humans will want to interact with your puppy and if they ask to hold your puppy, this is a good opportunity to socialize your puppy and show them that humans are friendly.

Do not let others (especially young children) play roughly with your puppy or squeal at them in a high-pitched voices because this can be very frightening for a sensitive young puppy, such as the Chiweenie.

As well, you do not want to teach your puppy that humans are a source of crazy, excited energy.

Be especially careful when introducing your puppy to young children who may accidentally hurt your puppy, because you don't want your dog to become fearful of children as this could lead to aggression issues later on in life.

Explain to children that your Chiweenie puppy is very young and that they must be calm and gentle when playing or interacting in any way.

3. Within Different Environments

It can be a big mistake not to take the time to introduce your Chiweenie puppy to a wide variety of different environments because when they are not comfortable with different sights and sounds, this could cause them possible trauma later in their adult life.

Be creative and take your puppy everywhere you can imagine when they are young so that no matter where they travel, whether strolling a noisy city sidewalk or along quiet seashore, they will be equally comfortable.

Don't make the mistake of only taking your Chiweenie puppy into areas where you live and will always travel because they need to also be comfortable visiting areas you might not often visit, such as noisy construction sites, airports or a shopping area across town.

Your puppy needs to see all sorts of sights, sounds and situations so that they will not become fearful should they need to travel with you to any of these areas.

Your Chiweenie puppy will take their cues from you, which means that when you are calm and in control of every situation, they will learn to be the same because they will trust your lead.

For instance, put your puppy in their Sherpa bag and take them to the airport where they can watch people and hear planes landing and taking off.

Take them to a local park where they can see a baseball game, or take them to the local zoo or farm and let them get a close up look at horses, pigs and ducks.

4. Loud Noises

Many dogs can show extreme fear of loud noises, such as fireworks or thunderstorms.

If you take the time to desensitize your Chiweenie to these types of noises when they are very young, it will be much easier on them during stormy weather or holidays such as Halloween or New Year's when fireworks are often a part of the festivities.

You can purchase CD's that are a collection of unusual sounds, such as vacuums or hoovers, airplanes, people clapping hands, and more, that you can play while working in your kitchen or relaxing in your living room or lounge.

When you play these sounds and pretend that everything is normal, the next time your puppy or dog hears these types of sounds elsewhere, they will not become upset or agitated because they have learned to ignore them.

Also make sure that you get your young puppy used to the sounds of thunder and fireworks at an early age because these types of shrieking, crashing, banging and popping sounds of fireworks or thunder can be so traumatic and unsettling for many dogs, that sometimes, no matter how much you try to calm your dog, or pretend that everything is fine, there is little you can do.

Some dogs literally lose their minds when they hear the loud popping or screeching noises of fireworks and start running or trying to hide and you cannot communicate with them at all.

Make sure that your dog cannot harm itself trying to escape from these types of noises, and if possible, calmly hold them until they begin to relax.

If your dog loses it's mind when it hears these types of noises, simply avoid taking them anywhere near fireworks and if at times when they might hear these noises going off outside, play your inside music or TV louder than you might normally, to help disguise the exterior noise of fireworks or thunder.

As well, some dogs will respond well to wearing a *"ThunderShirt"* which is specifically designed to alleviate anxiety or trauma associated with loud rumbling, popping or banging noises.

The idea behind the design of the ThunderShirt is that the gentle pressure it creates is similar to a hug that, for some dogs, has a calming effect.

Do not underestimate the importance of taking the time to continually (not just when they are puppies) socialize and desensitize your puppy to all manner of sights, sounds individuals and locations because to do so will be teaching them to be a calm and well balanced member of your family that will quietly follow you in every situation.

Chapter 15: Training

1. Trainability

As the Chiweenie has two relatively intelligent parents, they will almost undoubtedly also be an intelligent and fairly easy to train dog.

When taught with positive reinforcement, they will be eager learners who will easily excel at anything you have the time and patience to teach.

No matter what you decide to teach your Chiweenie, always train with patience and kindness and NEVER yell, hit or punish a dog during training, or at any time for that matter.

Using harsh, mean or loud training methods could frighten a Chiweenie and cause them to shut down. As well, any sort of harsh treatment will cause your friendly and sensitive Chiweenie to lose trust and respect of you, and they could also learn to fear you, which is NOT the type of relationship you want to have with your dog.

All training sessions should be happy and fun filled with plenty of rewards and positive reinforcement, which will ensure that your Chiweenie is an excellent student who looks forward to learning new commands and tricks.

The Chiweenie can be very skillful in many different forms of advanced dog sports, including agility, obedience, freestyle dance, rally, and more.

2. Puppy Training Basics

Most humans believe that they need to take their young dog to puppy classes, and generally speaking, this is a good idea for any young Chiweenie (after they have had their vaccinations), because it will help to get them socialized.

Beyond puppy classes for socializations reasons, hiring a professional dog whisperer for personalized private sessions to train the humans may be far more valuable than training situations where there are multiple dogs and humans together in one class as this can be very distracting for everyone concerned.

a) Three Most Important Words

"Come", **"Sit"** and **"Stay"** will be the three most important words you will ever teach your Chiweenie puppy.

These three basic commands will ensure that your Chiweenie remains safe in almost every circumstance.

For instance, when your puppy correctly learns the "Come" command, you can always quickly bring them back to your side if you should see danger be approaching.

When you teach your Chiweenie puppy the "Sit" and "Stay" commands you will be further establishing your leadership role. A puppy who understands that their human guardian is their leader will be a safe and happy follower.

b) Choosing a Discipline Sound

Choosing a *"discipline sound"* that will be the same for every human family member will make it much easier for your puppy to learn what they can or cannot do and will be very useful when warning your Chiweenie puppy before they engage in unwanted behavior.

The best types of sounds are short and sharp so that you and your family members can quickly say them and so that the sound will immediately get the attention of your Chiweenie puppy because you want to be able to easily interrupt them when they are about to make a mistake.

It doesn't really matter what the sound is, so long as everyone in the family is consistent.

A sound that is very effective for most puppies and dogs is a simple *"UH"* sound said sharply and with emphasis.

Most puppies and dogs respond immediately to this sound and if caught in the middle of doing something they are not supposed to be doing will quickly stop and give you their attention or back away from what they were doing.

3. Beginner Leash Lesson

Equipment: 4 or 6-foot leash, Martingale training collar.

The most important ongoing bonding exercise you will experience with your new Chiweenie puppy is when you go out for your daily walks together.

Far, far too many people ignore this critical, multi-tasking time that is not only important for your puppy's exercise, it fulfills a multitude of their needs, including:

- exercising their body
- fulfilling their natural roaming urges
- teaching them discipline, which engages their mind
- learning to follow, trust and respect you

As soon as you bring your new puppy home you will want to teach them how to walk at your side while on leash without pulling.

Every time your puppy needs to go out to relieve his or herself, slip on their collar and snap on that leash.

At first your Chiweenie puppy may struggle or fight against having a collar around their neck, because the sensation will be new to them. However, at the same time they will want to go with you, so exercise patience and encourage them to walk with you.

Be careful never to drag them, and if they pull backward and refuse to walk forward with you, simply stop for a moment, while keeping slight forward tension on the leash, until your Chiweenie puppy gives up and moves forward. Immediately reward them with your happy praise, and if they have a favorite treat, this can be an added incentive when teaching them to walk on their leash.

Always walk your puppy on your left side with the leash slack so that they learn that walking with you is a relaxing experience. Keep the leash short enough so that they do not have enough slack to get in front of you.

If they begin to create tension in the leash by pulling forward or to the side, simply stop moving, get them back beside you, and start over.

Be patient and consistent with your puppy and very soon they will understand exactly where their walking position is and will walk easily beside you without any pulling or leash tension.

Remember that walking with a new puppy is an exciting experience for them as they will want to sniff everything and explore their new world, so give them lots of understanding and don't expect them to be perfect all the time.

When your Chiweenie puppy is very young, and wanting to put everything in their mouths, walk then in a harness AND collar and leash, so that you can have a second leash attached to the harness.

This way, you will be able to easily lift them over cigarette butts or other garbage you may encounter while out walking. Once they grow out of the habit of tasting all manner of garbage, you can dispense with the harness and second leash.

4. Surviving Adolescence

The adolescent period in a young Chiweenie's life, between the ages of 6 and 12 months, is the transitional stage of both physical and psychological development when they are physically almost full grown in size, yet their minds are still developing and they are testing their boundaries and the limits that their human counterparts will endure.

This can be a dangerous time in a puppy's life because this is when they start to make decisions on their own which, if they do not receive the leadership they need from their human guardians, can lead to developing unwanted behaviors.

Learning how to make decisions on their own would be perfectly normal and desirable if your Chiweenie puppy was living in the wild, amongst a pack of dogs, because learning to make decisions would be necessary for their survival.

However, when living within a human environment, your puppy must always adhere to human rules and it will be up to their human guardians to continue their vigilant, watchful guidance in order to make sure that they do.

Many humans are lulled into a false sense of security when their new Chiweenie puppy reaches the age of approximately six months, because the puppy has been well socialized, they have been to puppy classes and long since been house trained.

The real truth is that the serious work is only now beginning and the humans and their new Chiweenie puppy could be in for a time of testing that could seriously challenge the relationship and leave the humans wondering if they made the right decision to share their home with a dog.

If the human side of the relationship is not prepared for this transitional time in their young dog's life, their patience may be seriously tried, and the relationship of trust and respect that has been previously built can be damaged, and could take considerable time to repair.

While not all adolescent puppies will experience a noticeable adolescent period of craziness, because every puppy is different, most young dogs do commonly exhibit at least some of the usual adolescent behaviors, including reverting to previous puppy behaviors.

Some of these adolescent behaviors might include destructive chewing of objects they have previously shown no interest in, selective hearing or ignoring previously learned commands, displaying aggressive behavior, jumping on everyone, barking at everything that moves, or reverting to relieving themselves in the house, even though they were house trained months ago.

Keeping your cool and recognizing these adolescent signs is the first step toward helping to make this transition period easier on your Chiweenie puppy and all family members.

The first step to take that can help keep raging hormones at bay, is to spay or neuter your Chiweenie puppy just prior to the onset of adolescence, at around four or five months of age.

While spaying or neutering a Chiweenie puppy will not entirely eliminate the adolescent phase, it will certainly help and at the same time will spare your puppy the added strain of both the physical and emotional changes that occur during sexual maturity.

As well, some female puppies will become extremely aggressive toward other dogs during a heat, and non-neutered males may become territorially aggressive and pick fights with other males.

Once your Chiweenie puppy has been spayed or neutered, you will want to become more active with your young dog, both mentally and physically by providing them with continued and more complex disciplined exercises.

This can be accomplished by enrolling your adolescent Chiweenie in a dog whispering session or more advanced training class, which will help them to continue their socialization skills while also developing their brain.

Even though it may be more difficult to train during this period, having the assistance of a professional and continuing the experience of ongoing socialization amongst other dogs of a similar size can be invaluable, as this is the time when many young dogs begin to show signs of antisocial behavior with other dogs as well as unknown humans.

When your Chiweenie is provided with sufficient daily exercise and continued socialization with unfamiliar dogs, people and places that provides interest and expands their mind, they will be able to transition through the adolescent stage of their life much more seamlessly.

5. Releasing Energy

The adolescent period in a puppy's life is a time of boundless energy and you will need to find ways to safely allow them to release this energy every day.

Since most humans cannot walk nearly fast enough to accommodate the needs of an energetic puppy, you will first want to walk your Chiweenie beside you on leash, and then find a safe place where they can run off leash, either chasing a ball, retrieving a Frisbee or playing and running in an enclosed area with other similar sized dogs where you can always supervise.

6. The Unruly Adolescent

If your Chiweenie puppy happens to be especially unruly during their adolescent phase, you will need to simply limit their opportunities for making mistakes.

For instance, a puppy who is digging up the yard, or chewing up just about anything they can get their teeth on will need to be closely supervised so that you can direct their energy into less harmful pursuits.

It does absolutely no good to yell at your Chiweenie puppy for engaging in behavior you are not happy with, and in fact, yelling or getting angry will only desensitize your young dog from listening to any of your commands.

Further, although you may eventually get the results you want, if you yell loud enough, your puppy will then be reacting out of fear, rather than respect, and this will be damaging to your relationship.

Displaying calm, yet assertive energy is the ONLY energy that works well to help your adolescent puppy understand what is required of them.

All other human emotions (frustration, anger, impatience, sadness, excitement) are "read" by puppies and dogs as being unstable, and not only will the smart and sensitive Chiweenie not understand these emotions, they will not respect you for displaying these types of unstable energies.

An extremely rambunctious adolescent Chiweenie may need to have their free run of the house curtailed so that they are confined to areas where you can easily supervise them.

Make sure they are within eyesight at all times, so that if they do find an opportunity to make a mistake, you can quickly show them what is permitted and what is not.
Adolescence may also be a time when you might have to insist that your young Chiweenie sleeps in their crate with the door closed whenever you cannot supervise, as well as at bedtime so they continue to understand that you have firm rules.

As well, keeping on top of house training is also a good idea during the adolescent period of your puppy's life because some adolescent puppies may become stubborn and forget that they are already house trained.

This means actually taking the time to be involved in the process by leashing up your Chiweenie and physically taking them outside whenever they need to relieve themselves. This sort of a routine is also a disciplined exercise that will help to reinforce in your puppy's mind, that you are the boss.

Too many humans with convenient yards simply do not participate at all in the bathroom routine of their young dogs and thereby miss out on endless opportunities to reinforce who is the boss.

7. Rewarding Unwanted Behavior

Often humans make the mistake of accidentally rewarding unwanted behaviors.

It is very important to recognize that any attention paid to an overly excited, out of control, adolescent puppy, even negative attention, is likely going to be rewarding for your puppy.

Therefore, when you engage with an out of control Chiweenie puppy, you end up actually rewarding them, which will encourage them to continue more of this unwanted behavior.

Be aware that chasing after a puppy when they have taken something they are not supposed to have, picking them up when they are barking or showing aggression, pushing them off when they jump on you or other people, or yelling when they refuse to come when called, are all forms of attention that can actually be rewarding for most puppies.

As your Chiweenie's guardian, it will be your responsibility to provide calm and consistent structure for your puppy, which will include finding acceptable and safe ways to allow your puppy to vent their energy without being destructive or harmful to property, other dogs, humans, or the actual puppy.

Activities that create or encourage an overly excited Chiweenie puppy, such as rough games of tug-o-war, or wild games of chase through the living room, should be immediately curtailed, so that your adolescent puppy learns how to control their energy and play quietly and appropriately without jumping on everyone or engaging in barking or mouthy behavior.

Further, if your adolescent Chiweenie puppy displays excited energy simply from being petted by yourself, your family members or any visitors, you will need to teach yourself, your family and your friends to ignore your puppy until they calm down. Otherwise, you will be teaching your Chiweenie puppy that the touch of humans mean excitement.

For instance, when you continue to engage with an overly excited puppy, you are rewarding them for out of control behavior and literally teaching them that when they see humans, you want them to display excited energy.

Worse, once your puppy has learned that humans are a source of excitement, you will then have to work very long and hard to reverse this behavior.

Children are often a source of excitement that can cause an adolescent puppy to be extremely wound up.

Do not allow your children to engage with an adolescent Chiweenie puppy unless you are there to supervise and teach the children appropriate and calm ways to interact with the puppy. In order to keep everyone safe, it is very important that your Chiweenie puppy learn at an early age that neither children nor adults are sources of excitement.

You can help develop the mind of an adolescent Chiweenie and the minds of growing children at the same time by teaching children that your puppy needs structured walks and by showing them how to play fetch, search, hide and seek, or how to teach the Chiweenie puppy simple tricks and obedience skills that will be fun and positive interaction for everyone.

8. Back to Basics

When your puppy is going through what could be a belligerent and trying adolescence, when it seems that they have forgotten everything they may have learned so far, this is an especially good time to revisit the simple "Sit" command.

Now, in order to help re-establish your leadership role, you will want to ask your Chiweenie puppy to sit at every opportunity.

The simple act of "sitting" will help to calm an excited mind and will get your puppy's focus back on you.

9. Sit and More Sit

Every time you take your Chiweenie out for a walk, which is usually a cause of excitement, get into the habit of asking them to sit while you put on their leash — then ask them to sit and calmly wait while you put on your shoes or jacket — after you approach the door, ask them to sit again while you open the door — after you are on the other side of the door — ask them to sit again while you lock the door.

If there are stairs or landings involved, ask them to sit at the top and also again at the bottom.

Every time you arrive at street intersection or a crosswalk, ask your Chiweenie puppy to sit again, and do this in reverse when coming back home.

Also, every time you stop during your walk to speak to a neighbor, greet a friend or admire the view, ask your puppy to sit.

Every time you ask your young dog to sit for you, they are learning several things all at once — that they must remain calm, that you are the boss and that they must respect you as their leader.

Also, a sitting puppy is much more easy to control than one standing at the alert, ready to bolt out the door or jump on someone.

Once your puppy is reliably sitting for you at least 50% of the time with voice command, also include the hand signal for "Sit", so that they will hear the word and also see the signal.

While you can use any hand signal, the universal hand signal for "Sit" is:

Right arm (palm open facing upward) parallel to the floor, and then raising your arm, while bent at the elbow toward your right shoulder.

Once your Chiweenie is sitting reliable for you, remove the verbal "Sit" and replace it with the hand signal.

It's important to begin teaching hand signals during the adolescent stage of your puppy's life, because this will also help them to communicate in a way that is more natural for a dog — by watching you and feeling your energy, rather than always having to hear you speak a command.

As well, because the action of sitting helps to calm the mind of an excited puppy (or dog), teaching your puppy the "Sit" command is a very important part of their daily interactions with your family members as well as people you may meet when out on a walk.

When you ask your puppy to "Sit" before you interact in any way with them, before you go out or in every door, before you feed them, etc., you are helping to quiet their mind, while making it more difficult for them to jump, lunge or disappear out a door.

The adolescent stage in a young dog's life is the perfect time to begin teaching hand signals for all your common commands, because they must look at you to understand what is expected of them, and when they are looking at you, they are more focused and less likely to take matters into their own paws.

10. Giving Up is Not an Option

Too often we humans get frustrated and give up on our dogs when they change from being the cute, cuddly and mostly obedient little puppy they once were, and become all kinds of trouble you never bargained for, as they grow into their adolescent stage.

Often times, it will be during the confusing adolescent stage of a dog's life that they find themselves abandoned and behind bars as their humans who promised to love and protect them, leave their once loved fur friend at the local pound or SPCA.

First of all, not all dogs go through a crazy adolescent period, and secondly, even if they do, please read this section carefully humans, because you can live through puppy adolescence and come out the other side relatively unscathed and a much more knowledgeable and patient guardian.

Congratulations are in order because you've been successful with potty training your young Chiweenie puppy and with teaching them to sleep in their own kennel at night.

Further, you've lived through the teething troubles, the chewing and the hand nipping and you no longer have to get up at 3:00 a.m. to let your puppy out to relieve itself.

As well, you've taught your Chiweenie puppy their first few basic commands, and socialized them with many other dogs, people and places, so you should feel proud of all your accomplishments and the leaps and bounds you and your puppy have accomplished together over the last several months.

Even though your adolescent puppy may be starting to act like a Tasmanian devil, and you may be having second thoughts, now is not the time to give up on them and yourself just because it may seem like someone switched your dog when you weren't looking.

Now is the time to remain calmly consistent and persistent, and to know that you will eventually be able to enjoy the happy rewards of all your puppy raising diligence.

Yes, it can be quite a shock when what used to be your well behaved little darling who never chewed anything they weren't supposed to suddenly takes it into their head eat all the tassels off your Persian rug or chew through a seat belt in your vehicle during the short 15 minutes you were shopping.

Even more disconcerting might be when your previously obedient and loving Chiweenie puppy, who always listened to your directions, suddenly appears to have gone deaf and can't remember their name when you call them to follow you inside the house, and instead they take off running after a cat three blocks away.

And then, what happened to that quiet little puppy that never appeared to have a mean bone in their body that now spends most of their time at the window barking and growling at everything and everyone passing by?

Welcome to the world of canine adolescence where it appears that your puppy has turned into some sort of monster and all your previous hard work was for naught.

Of course, this dramatic switch from being the world's best puppy into the monster you can no longer control is not true for all puppies, as every puppy is unique.

However, being prepared for the worst will help you ride any impending storm and get you both out the other side where you can enjoy an even closer relationship than you previously had.

The adolescent phase may be very subtle for your Chiweenie puppy or on the other hand, it may be so dramatic that you're starting to feel guilty every time you drive past the local SPCA or dog pound because thoughts of rehoming are running through your head.

If you are at the stage with your puppy that you are having great difficulties and wondering if you made the right decision to share your home with a dog, rest assured that puppy adolescence is a normal phase of their development, which can be managed, and which will definitely pass.

As well, if you are finding yourself totally overwhelmed, there are many professionals who can provide valuable assistance to help you through this stage of your Chiweenie puppy's development.

For most puppies, adolescence will begin between the ages of five and seven months and this is also the time that you need to be making an appointment at your veterinarian's office to have your puppy spayed or neutered.

Although neutering or spaying will not prevent adolescent behavior entirely, it can certainly reduce the intensity of it, as during this period there are hormonal changes occurring that will affect your puppy's behavior.

While it's usually hormones that are the major cause of behavioral changes in your adolescent puppy, there are also physical changes occurring at the same time that you may not be aware of.

For instance, your puppy will be going through physical growth spurts which might be causing them some pain, as well as changes related to growth in their brain while your puppy's cerebral cortex becomes more involved in thinking for itself.

Usually, during this time of brain growth, a puppy will be trying to make choices for themself, and may or may not yet be capable of making the right choices. This is why their behavior can appear to be quite erratic.

During the early adolescent period of brain development in your Chiweenie puppy, the signals sometimes get mixed up and rerouted, which can result in the perplexing responses you might notice, when for instance, you ask you puppy to sit and they stare dumbly at you, even though they learned this command months ago.

Don't worry because your previous training will return.

11. Re-visit Basic First Commands

All that's necessary for effectively teaching your puppy their basic first commands is a calm, consistent approach, combined with your endless patience.

Many puppies are ready to begin training at about 10 to 12 weeks of age, however, be careful not to overdo it when they are less than six months of age, as their attention span will be short.

Make your training sessions no more than 5 or 10 minutes, positive and pleasant with lots of praise and/or treats so that your puppy will be looking forward to their next session.

Also, introduce the hand signals that go along with the verbal commands so that once they learn both, you can remove the verbal commands in favor of just hand signals.

a) Come

While the intelligent Chiweenie puppy will be capable of learning commands and tricks at a young age, the first and most important command you need to teach your puppy is the recall, or *"Come"* command.

The hand signal for "Come" is your arms spread wide open. This is a command they can see from a great distance.

Begin the "Come" command inside your home. Go into a larger room, such as your living room area. Place your puppy in front of you and attach their leash or a longer line to their Martingale collar, while you back away from them a few feet.

Say the command "Come" in an excited, happy voice and hold your arms open wide. If they do not immediately come to you, gently give a tug on the leash so that they understand that they are supposed to move toward you. When they come to you praise them and give a treat they really enjoy.

Once your puppy can accomplish a "Come" command almost every time inside your home, you can then graduate them to a nearby park or quiet outside area where you will repeat the process.

You may want to purchase an extra long line (25 or 50 feet) so that you are always attached to your Chiweenie puppy and can encourage them in the right direction should they become distracted.

b) Sit

The "Sit" and "Stay" commands are both easy commands to teach that will help to keep your Chiweenie puppy safe and out of danger in most every circumstance.

Find a quiet time to teach these commands when your puppy is not overly tired.

Ask your puppy to "Sit" and if they do not yet understand the command, show them what you mean by gently squeezing with your thumb and middle finger, the area across the back that joins with their back legs.

Do not just push them down into a sit as this can cause damage to their back or joints. When they sit, give them a treat and praise them.

When you say the word "Sit", at the same time show them the hand signal for this command, which is bending your arm at the elbow and raising your right hand, palm open facing upward, toward your shoulder.

c) Stay

Once your Chiweenie puppy can reliably "Sit", say the word "Stay" and hold your outstretched arm, palm open toward their head and back away a few steps.

If they try to follow, calmly say "No" and put them back into "Sit". Give a treat and then say again, "Stay" with the hand signal and back away a few steps.

Once your puppy is sitting and staying, you can then ask them to "Come". Don't forget to use the open arms hand signal for "Come." Be a little excited with the "Come" command so that your puppy will always enjoy correctly responding and immediately returning to you.

Practice these three basic commands everywhere you go, and use the "Sit" command every time you go for a walk, before you open the door, after you are on the other side of the door, before you go down the stairs, once you are at the bottom of the stairs, and every time you stop when you are on your walk, and pretty soon you will have a puppy who automatically sits whenever you stop moving.

As your puppy gets older, and their attention span increases, you will be able to train for longer periods of time.

12. Hand Signals

Hand signal training is by far the most useful and efficient training method for every dog, including the Chiweenie.

This is because all too often we inundate our canine companions with a great deal of chatter and noise that they really do not understand because English is not their first language.

Contrary to what some humans might think, the first language of a Chiweenie, or any dog, is a combination of sensing energy and watching body language, which requires no spoken word or sound.

Therefore, when we humans take the time to teach our dog hand signals for all their basic commands, we are communicating with them at a level they instinctively understand, plus we are helping them to become a focused follower, as they must watch us to understand what is required of them.

a) Come

Come: you can kneel down for this command or stay standing. Open your arms wide like you are hugging a very large tree. This hand signal can be seen from a long distance.

When first teaching hand signals to your Chiweenie, always show the hand signal for the command at the same time you say the word.

If they are totally ignoring the command, it will be time to incorporate a lunge line, which is a very long leash to help you teach the "Come" command.

Simply attach a 20-foot line to their collar and let them sniff about in a large yard or at your neighborhood park.

At your leisure, firmly ask them to "Come" and show the hand signal. If they do not immediately come to you, give a firm tug with the lunge line, so that they understand what you are asking of them.

If they still do not "Come" toward you, simply reel them in until they are in front of you. Then let them wander about again, until you are ready to ask them to "Come".

Repeat this process until your Chiweenie responds correctly at least 80% of the time. You can also reinforce the command by giving a treat when they come back to you when asked. Always ask them to "Sit" when they return to you.

b) Sit

Sit: right arm (palm open facing upward) parallel to the floor, and then raise your arm, while bent at the elbow toward your shoulder.

Sit is a very simple, yet extremely valuable command for all puppies and dogs.

If your dog is not sitting on command, try holding a treat above and slightly behind their head, so that when they look up for it they may automatically sit to see it.

Slowly remove the treats as reward and replace the treat with a "life reward", such as a chest rub or a scratch behind the ears and your happy smile.

If your Chiweenie is not particularly treat motivated, lift up and slightly back on the leash when asking them to sit (stand in front of them), and if they still are having difficulties, reach down with your free hand, place it across your dog's back at the place where the back legs join the hip and gently squeeze.

Remember -- Do NOT simply push down on your dog's back to force their hind legs to collapse under them as this pressure could harm their spine or leg joints.

c) Stay

Stay: right armed fully extended toward your dog's head, palm open, hand bent up at the wrist.

Once your Chiweenie is in the "Sit" position, ask them to "Stay" with both the verbal cue and the hand signal.

TIP: if you are right-handed, use your right arm and hand for the signal, and if you are left-handed, use your left arm and hand for the signal. Using your dominant hand will be much more effective because your strongest energy emanates from the palm of your dominant hand.

While your dog is sitting and staying, slowly back away from them. If they move from their position, calmly put them back into Sit and ask them to "Stay" again, using both the verbal cue and the hand signal.

Continue to practice this until your dog understands that you want them to stay sitting and not move toward you.

With all commands, when your Chiweenie is just learning, be patient and always reward them with a treat and your happy praise for a job well done.

13. Simple Tricks

When teaching your Chiweenie tricks, in order to give them extra incentive, find a treat that they really like, and give the treat as rewards and to help solidify a good performance.

Most dogs will be extra attentive during training sessions when they know that they will be rewarded with their favorite treats.

If your Chiweenie is less than six months old when you begin teaching them tricks, keep your training sessions short (no more than 5 or 10 minutes) and fun, and as they become adults, you can extend your sessions as they will be able to maintain their focus for longer periods of time.

a) Shake a Paw

Who doesn't love a dog that knows how to shake a paw? This is one of the easiest tricks to teach your Chiweenie.

TIP: most dogs are naturally either right or left pawed. If you know which paw your dog favors, ask them to shake this paw.

Find a quiet place to practice, without noisy distractions or other pets, and stand or sit in front of your dog. Place them in the sitting position and have a treat in your left hand.

Say the command *"Shake"* while putting your right hand behind their left or right paw and pulling the paw gently toward yourself until you are holding their paw in your hand. Immediately praise them and give them the treat.

Most dogs will learn the "Shake" trick very quickly, and very soon, once you put out your hand, your Chiweenie will immediately lift their paw and put it into your hand, without your assistance or any verbal cue.

Practice every day until they are 100% reliable with this trick, and then it will be time to add another trick to their repertoire.

b) Roll Over

You will find that just like your Chiweenie is naturally either right or left pawed, that they will also naturally want to roll either to the right or the left side. Take advantage of this by asking your dog to roll to the side they naturally prefer.

Sit with your dog on the floor and put them in a lie down position. Hold a treat in your hand and place it close to their nose without allowing them to grab it, and while they are in the lying position, move the treat to the right or left side of their head so that they have to roll over to get to it.

You will very quickly see which side they want to naturally roll to, and once you see this, move the treat to this side. Once they roll over to this side, immediately give them the treat and praise them.

You can say the verbal cue *"Over"* while you demonstrate the hand signal motion (moving your right hand in a circular motion) or moving the treat from one side of their head to the other with a half circle motion.

Roll Over: moving your right or left arm/hand in a small circular motion, in the direction you wish your dog to roll toward.

Once your Chiweenie can roll over every time you ask, it will be time to teach them another trick.

c) Sit Pretty

While this trick is a little more complicated, and most dogs pick up on it very quickly, remember that every dog is different so always exercise patience.

Find a quiet space with few distractions and sit or stand in front of your dog and ask them to "Sit".

Have a treat nearby (on a countertop or table) and when they sit, use both of your hands to lift up their front paws into the sitting pretty position, while saying the command *"Sit Pretty"*. Help them balance in this position while you praise them and give them the treat.

Once your Chiweenie can do the balancing part of the trick quite easily without your help, sit or stand in front of your dog while asking them to *"Sit Pretty"* and hold the treat above their head, at the level their nose would be when they sit pretty.

TIP: when first beginning this trick, place your Chiweenie beside a wall so they can use the wall to help them balance.

If they attempt to stand on their back legs to get the treat, you may be holding the treat too high, which will encourage them to stand on their back legs to reach it. Go back to the first step and put them back into the *"Sit"* position and again lift their paws while their backside remains on the floor.

Sit Pretty: hold your straight arm, fully extended, over your dog's head with a closed fist.

Make this a fun and entertaining time for your Chiweenie and practice a few times every day until they can *"Sit Pretty"* on hand signal command every time you ask.

A young Chiweenie puppy should be able to easily learn these basic tricks before they are six months old and when you are patient and make your training sessions short and fun for your dog, they will be eager to learn more.

14. Adult Training

The Chiweenie is and intelligent breed that will be skillful in many different dog sports, such as agility, obedience, or freestyle dance.

When your Chiweenie is a full grown adult (approximately two years of age), you will definitely want to begin more complicated or advanced training sessions.

They will enjoy it and when you have the desire and patience, there is no end to the tricks or routines you can teach a willing Chiweenie.

For instance, you may wish to teach your adult Chiweenie more advanced tricks, such as how to dance, or the opposite sided paw shakes or roll overs, which are more difficult than you might expect.

If you and your Chiweenie are really enjoying learning new tricks together, you might want to advance to teaching them the *"commando crawl"*, how to *"speak"* or to *"jump through the human hoop"*.

All of these tricks and many more are fun to teach and will exercise both your Chiweenie's mind and body by taking advantage of their natural ability to excel as an entertaining circus performer.

As well, the more control you have over your Chiweenie, the easier it will be to teach them a fun sport, such as Agility or Freestyle dance.

The only restriction to how far you can go with training your adult Chiweenie will be your imagination and their personal ability or desire to perform.

15. Behavioral Issues

It can be difficult, if not impossible to generalize or speculate with respect to alleviating possible behavioral issues or problems because, in most cases, a dog suffering from behavioral issues requires the assistance of a dog whisperer or dog psychologist.

When reading anything about how to prevent or cure behavioral issues, please be aware that behavioral problems most often cannot be properly assessed or cured by reading a book.

The reason for this is because there are just too many variables and unique situations, individual dogs, individual humans, unique circumstances, and endless reasons why they may have developed any particular behavioral issue.

Therefore, without knowing the dog's particulars and all the history of what has transpired between the Chiweenie and their guardian that came before, attempting to write about how to cure a particular issue will be no more than a best guess.

This is why someone whose dog is suffering from a specific behavioral issue that is in turn, at the least embarrassing, or at the worst, driving the humans and the entire neighborhood crazy, must be properly addressed by engaging the services of a professional dog whisperer (psychologist or behaviorist) who can ask many questions, properly assess the situation and then design a unique plan for alleviating the problem.

16. Overheating

Be very careful, when training or walking your Chiweenie outside during hot weather that you do not allow them to become overheated.
Always carry water with you to help keep them hydrated.

TIP: if your Chiweenie has a coat that is darker colored, you can easily help to keep them cooler on hot, sunny days by having them wear a light weight vest that is a lighter color than their own coat.

Remember that they are close to heated pavement or road surface, which means that on a hot, sunny day, they will literally be heated from both the bottom and the top.

If the pavement is very hot, do not allow them to walk on it. Instead, take them to a grassy area for their exercise.

Chapter 16: Poisonous Foods & Plants

1. Poisonous Foods

While some dogs are smart enough not to want to eat foods that can harm or kill them, other canine companions will eat absolutely anything they can get their teeth on.

As conscientious guardians for our fur friends, it will always be our responsibility to make certain that when we share our homes with a dog, we never leave foods that could be toxic or lethal to them easily within their reach.

While there are many foods that can be toxic to a Chiweenie, the following alphabetical list contains some of the more common foods that can seriously harm or even kill our dogs including:

Bread Dough: if your dog eats bread dough, their body heat will cause the dough to rise inside the stomach. As the dough expands during the rising process, alcohol is produced.

Dogs who have eaten bread dough may experience stomach bloating, abdominal pain, vomiting, disorientation and depression. Because bread dough can rise to many times its original size, eating only a small amount will cause a problem for any dog.

Broccoli: the toxic ingredient in broccoli is isothiocynate. While it may cause stomach upset, it probably won't be very harmful unless the amount eaten is more than 10% of the dog's total daily diet.

Chocolate: contains theobromine, a chemical that is toxic to dogs in large enough quantities. Chocolate also contains caffeine, which is found in coffee, tea, and certain soft drinks. Different types of chocolate contain different amounts of theobromine and caffeine.

For example, dark chocolate and baking chocolate or cocoa powder contain more of these compounds than milk chocolate does, therefore, a dog would need to eat more milk chocolate in order to become ill.

However, even a few ounces of chocolate can be enough to cause illness or death in a puppy or smaller dog, like the Chiweenie, therefore, no amount or type of chocolate should be considered safe for a dog to eat.

Chocolate toxicity can cause vomiting, diarrhea, rapid or irregular heart rate, restlessness, muscle tremors, and seizures. Death can occur within 24 hours of eating.

During many holidays such as Christmas, New Year's, Valentine's, Easter and Halloween, chocolate is often more easily accessible to curious dogs, especially from children who are not so careful with where they might keep their Halloween or Easter egg stash and who are an easy mark for a hungry dog.

In some cases, people unwittingly poison their dogs by offering them chocolate as a treat or leaving chocolate cookies or frosted cake easily within licking distance.

Caffeine: beverages containing caffeine, such as soda, tea, coffee, and chocolate, act as a stimulant and can accelerate your dog's heartbeat to a dangerous level. Dogs eating caffeine have been known to have seizures, some of which are fatal.

Cooked Bones: can be extremely hazardous for a dog because the bones become brittle when cooked which causes them to splinter when the dog chews on them.

The splinters have sharp edges that have been known to become stuck in the teeth, and cause choking when caught in the throat or create a rupture or puncture of the stomach lining or intestinal tract.

Especially dangerous are cooked turkey and chicken legs, ham, pork chop and veal bones. Symptoms of choking include:

- Pale or blue gums
- Gasping open-mouthed breathing
- Pawing at the face
- Slow, shallow breathing
- Falling unconscious with dilated pupils

Grapes and Raisins: can cause acute (sudden) kidney failure in dogs. While it is not known what the toxic agent is in this fruit, clinical signs can occur within 24 hours of eating and include vomiting, diarrhea, and lethargy (tiredness).

Other signs of illness caused from eating grapes or raisins relate to the eventual shutdown of kidney functioning.

Garlic and Onions: contain chemicals that damage red blood cells by rupturing them so that they lose their ability to carry oxygen effectively, which leaves the dog short of oxygen, causing what is called *"hemolytic anemia"*.

Poisoning can occur with a single ingestion of large quantities of garlic or onions or with repeated meals containing small amounts.

Cooking does not reduce the potential toxicity of onions and garlic.

NOTE: fresh, cooked, and/or powdered garlic or onions are commonly found in baby food, which is sometimes given to dogs when they are sick, therefore, be certain to carefully read food labels before feeding to your Chiweenie.

Macadamia Nuts: are commonly found in candies and chocolates. Although the mechanism of macadamia nut toxicity is not well understood, the clinical signs in dogs having eaten these nuts include depression, weakness, vomiting, tremors, joint pain, and pale gums.

Signs can occur within 12 hours after eating. In some cases, symptoms can resolve themselves without treatment within 24 to 48 hours, however, keeping a close eye on your Chiweenie will be strongly recommended.

Mushrooms: mushroom poisoning can be fatal if certain species of mushrooms are eaten.

The most commonly reported severely toxic species of mushroom in the US is Amanita phalloides (Death Cap mushroom), which is also quite a common species found in most parts of Britain. Other Amanita species are also toxic.

This deadly mushroom is often found growing in grassy or wooded areas near various deciduous and coniferous trees, which mean that if you're out walking with your Chiweenie in the woods, they could easily find these mushrooms.

Eating them can cause severe liver disease and neurological disorders. If you suspect your dog has eaten these mushrooms, immediately take them to your veterinarian, as the recommended treatment is to induce vomiting and to give activated charcoal. Further treatment for liver disease may also be necessary.

Pits and Seeds: many seeds and pits found in a variety of fruits, including apples, apricots, cherries, pears and plums, contain cyanogenic glycosides that can cause cyanide poisoning in your Chiweenie.

The symptoms of cyanide poisoning usually occur within 15-20 minutes to a few hours after eating and symptoms can include initial excitement, followed by rapid respiration rate, salivation, voiding of urine and feces, vomiting, muscle spasm, staggering, and coma before death.

Dogs suffering from cyanide poisoning that live more than 2 hours after onset of symptoms will usually recover.

Raw Salmon or Trout: Salmon Poisoning Disease (SPD) can be a problem for anyone who goes fishing with their dog, or feeds their dog a raw meat diet that includes raw salmon or trout.

When a snail is infected and then is eaten by the fish, as part of the food chain, the dog is exposed when it eats the infected fish.

A sudden onset of symptoms can occur 5-7 days after eating the infected fish. In the acute stages, gastrointestinal symptoms are quite similar to canine parvovirus.

SPD has a mortality rate of up to 90%, can be diagnosed with a fecal sample and is treatable if caught in time.

Prevention is simple, cook all fish before feeding it to your Chiweenie and immediately see your veterinarian if you suspect that your dog has eaten raw salmon or trout.

Tobacco: all forms of tobacco, including patches, nicotine gum and chewing tobacco can be fatal to dogs if eaten.

Signs of poisoning can appear within an hour and include hyperactivity, salivation, panting, vomiting and diarrhea. Advanced signs include muscle weakness, twitching, collapse, coma, increased heart rate and eventually cardiac arrest.

Never leave tobacco products within reach of your Chiweenie, and be careful not to let them pick up discarded cigarette butts when they are young puppies.

If you suspect your dog has eaten any of these, seek immediate veterinary help.

TIP: when your Chiweenie is a very young puppy, use a double leash, collar and harness arrangement, so that you can still teach them to walk on leash with a Martingale collar around their neck, but can also attach the second leash to their harness so that you can easily lift them over enticing cigarette butts or other toxic garbage they may be trying to eat during your walks.

Tomatoes: contain atropine, which can cause dilated pupils, tremors and irregular heartbeat. The highest concentration of atropine is found in the leaves and stems of tomato plants, next is the unripe (green) tomatoes, followed by the ripe tomato.

Xylitol: is an artificial sweetener found in products such as gum, candy, mints, toothpaste, and mouthwash that is recognized by the National Animal Poison Control Center to be a risk to dogs.

Xylitol is harmful to dogs because it causes a sudden release of insulin in the body that leads to hypoglycemia (low blood sugar). Xylitol can also cause liver damage in dogs.

Within 30 minutes after eating a product containing xylitol, the dog may vomit, be lethargic (tired), and/or be uncoordinated. However, some signs of toxicity can also be delayed for hours or even for a few days. Xylitol toxicity in dogs can be fatal if left untreated.

Please be aware that the above list is just some of the more common foods that can be toxic or fatal to our fur friends and that there are many other foods we should never be feeding our dogs.

If you have one of those dogs who will happily eat anything that looks or smells even slightly like food, be certain to keep these foods far away from your beloved Chiweenie and you'll help them to live a long and healthy life.

2. Poisonous Household Plants

Many common house plants are actually poisonous to our canine companions, and although many dogs simply will ignore house plants, some will attempt to eat anything, especially puppies who want to taste everything in their new world.

More than 700 plant species contain toxins that may harm or be fatal to puppies or dogs, depending on the size of the puppy or dog and how much they may eat. It will be especially important to be aware of household plants that could be toxic when you are sharing your home with a new puppy.

Following is a short list of the more common household plants, what they look like, the different names they are known by, and what symptoms would be apparent if your puppy or dog decides to eat them.

Aloe Plant: (medicine plant or Barbados aloe), is a very common succulent that is toxic to dogs. The toxic agent in this plant is Aloin.

This bitter yellow substance is found in most aloe species and may cause vomiting and/or reddish urine.

Asparagus Fern: (emerald feather, emerald fern, sprengeri fern, plumosa fern, lace fern). The toxic agent in this plant is sapogenin

— a steroid found in a variety of plants. Berries of this plant cause vomiting, diarrhea and/or abdominal pain or skin inflammation from repeated exposure.

Corn Plant: (cornstalk plant, dracaena, dragon tree, ribbon plant) is toxic to dogs. Saponin is the offensive chemical compound found in this plant. If the plant is eaten, vomiting (with or without blood), loss of appetite, depression and/or increased salivation can occur.

Cyclamen: (Sowbread) is a pretty, flowering plant that, if eaten, can cause increased salivation, vomiting and diarrhea. If a dog eats a large amount of the plant's tubers, which are usually found below the soil at the root — heart rhythm abnormalities, seizures and even death can occur.

Dieffenbachia: (dumb cane, tropic snow, exotica) contains a chemical that is a poisonous deterrent to animals. If the plant is eaten, oral irritation can occur, especially on the tongue and lips. This irritation can lead to increased salivation, difficulty swallowing and vomiting.

Elephant Ear: (caladium, taro, pai, ape, cape, via, via sori, malanga) contains a chemical similar to that found in dieffenbachia, therefore, a dog's toxic reaction to elephant ear is similar: oral irritation, increased salivation, difficulty swallowing and vomiting.

Heartleaf Philodendron: (horsehead philodendron, cordatum, fiddle leaf, panda plant, split-leaf philodendron, fruit salad plant, red emerald, red princess, saddle leaf), is a common, easy-to-grow houseplant that contains a chemical irritating to the mouth, tongue and lips of dogs. An affected dog may also experience increased salivation, vomiting and difficulty swallowing.

Jade Plant: (baby jade, dwarf rubber plant, jade tree, Chinese rubber plant, Japanese rubber plant, friendship tree). While the toxic property in this plant is unknown, eating it can cause depression, loss of coordination and, although more rare, slow heart rate.

Lilies: some plants of the lily family are toxic to dogs. The peace lily (also known as Mauna Loa) is toxic to dogs. Eating the peace lily or calla lily can cause irritation of the tongue and lips, increased salivation, difficulty swallowing and vomiting.

Satin Pothos: (silk pothos), if eaten by a dog, the plant may cause irritation to the mouth, lips and tongue, while the dog may also experience increased salivation, vomiting and/or difficulty swallowing.

The plants noted above are only a few of the more common household plants, and every conscientious Chiweenie guardian will want to educate themselves before bringing plants into the home that could be toxic to their canine companions.

3. Poison Proof Your Home

You can learn about many potentially toxic and poisonous sources both inside and outside your home by visiting the ASPCA Animal Poison Control Center website.

Always keep your veterinarian's emergency number in a place where you can quickly access it, as well as the Emergency Poison Control telephone number, in case you suspect that your dog may have been poisoned.

Knowing what to do if you suspect your dog may have been poisoned and being able to quickly contact the right people could save your Chiweenie's life.

If you keep toxic cleaning substances (including fertilizers, vermin or snail poisons and vehicle products) in your home or garage, always keep them behind closed doors.

As well, keep any medications where your Chiweenie can never get to them, and seriously consider eliminating the use of any and all toxic products, for the health of both yourself and your best friend.

4. Garden Plants

Please note that there are also many outdoor plants that can be toxic or poisonous to your Chiweenie, therefore, always check what plants are growing in your garden and if any may be harmful, remove them or make certain that your Chiweenie puppy or adult dog cannot eat them.

Cornell University, Department of Animal Science lists many different categories of poisonous plants affecting dogs, including house plants, flower garden plants, vegetable garden plants, plants found in swamps or moist areas, plants found in fields, trees and shrubs, plants found in wooded areas, and ornamental plants.

5. Why Does My Dog Eat Grass?

Also, be aware that many puppies and adult dogs will eat grass, just because. Perhaps they are curious, bored, or need a little fiber in their diet.

Remember that canines are natural scavengers always on the look out for something they can eat, and so long as the grass is healthy and has not been sprayed with toxic chemicals, this should not be a concern.

6. Animal Poison Control Centre

The ASPCA Animal Poison Control Center is staffed 24 hours a day, 365 days a year and is a valuable resource for learning about what plants are toxic and possibly poisonous to your dog.

a) USA Poison Emergency

Call: 1 (888) 426-4435

When calling the Poison Emergency number, a $65. US (£39.42) consultation fee may be applied to your credit card.

b) UK Poison Emergency

Call: 0800-213-6680 - Pet Poison Helpline (payable service)

Call: 0300 1234 999 - RSPCA

www.aspca.org = ASPCA Poison Control.

Chapter 17: Caring for Aging Dogs

1. What to Be Aware Of

As a result of many modern advances in veterinarian care, improvements in diet and nutrition and general knowledge concerning proper care of our canine companions, our dogs are able to enjoy longer, healthier lives.

As such, when caring for our canine companions, we need to be aware of behavioral and physical changes that will affect our dogs as they approach old age.

While each dog's individual health, genetics, and spirit will affect how old they seem, and they may remain quite active, a Chiweenie will be entering their senior years at around 8 to 10 years of age.

a) Physiological Changes

As our beloved canine companions enter into their senior years, they may be suffering from very similar, physical aging problems that affect us humans, such as pain, stiffness and arthritis, and inability to control their bowels and bladder.

Any of these problems will reduce a dog's willingness to want to exercise.

b) Behavioral Changes

Further, a senior Chiweenie may experience behavioral changes resulting from loss of hearing and sight, such as disorientation, fear or startle reactions and overall grumpiness from any number of physical problems that could be causing them pain whenever they move.

Just as research and science has improved our human quality of life in our senior years, the same is becoming true for our canine counterparts who are able to benefit from dietary supplements and pharmaceutical products to help them be as comfortable as possible in their senior years.

Of course, there will be some inconveniences associated with keeping a dog with advancing years around the home, however, your Chiweenie deserves no less than to spend their final days in your loving care after they have unconditionally given you their entire lives.

c) Geriatric Dogs

Being aware of the changes that are likely occurring in a senior dog will help you to better care for them during their geriatric years.

For instance, most dogs will experience hearing loss and visual impairment, and how you help them will depend upon which goes first (hearing or sight).

For instance, if a dog's hearing is compromised, then using more hand signals will be helpful.

Deaf dogs will still be able to hear louder noises and feel vibrations, therefore hand clapping, knocking on walls, doors or furniture, using a loud clicker or stomping your foot on the floor may be a way to get their attention.

If a senior dog loses their eyesight, most dogs will still be able to easily navigate their familiar surroundings, and you will only need to be extra watchful on their behalf when taking them to unfamiliar territory.

If they still have their hearing, you will be able to assist your dog with verbal cues and commands.

Dogs that have lost both their hearing and their sight will need to be close to you so that they can relax and not feel nervous, and so that you can communicate by touching parts of their body.

Generally speaking, even when a dog becomes blind and/or deaf, their powerful sense of smell is still functioning, which means that they will be able to smell where you are and navigate their environment by using their nose.

d) More Bathroom Breaks

Bathroom breaks may need to become more frequent in older dogs who may lose their ability to hold it for longer periods of time, so be prepared to be more watchful and to offer them opportunities to go outside more frequently during the day.

You may also want to place a pee pad near the door, in case they just can't hold it long enough, or if you have not already taught them to bathroom on an indoor potty patch, or pee pad, now may be the time for this alternative bathroom arrangement.

A dog who has been house trained for years will feel the shame and upset of not being able to hold it long enough to get to their regular bathroom location, so be kind and do whatever you need to do in order to help them not to have to feel bad about failing bowel or bladder control.

Our beloved canine companions may also begin to show signs of cognitive decline and changes in the way their brain functions, similar to what happens to humans suffering from Alzheimer's, where they start to wander about aimlessly, sometimes during the middle of the night.

Make sure that if this is happening with your Chiweenie at nighttime, that they cannot accidentally fall down stairs or harm themselves in any way.

Being aware that an aging Chiweenie will be experiencing many symptoms that are similar to an aging human will help you to understand how best to keep them safe and as comfortable as possible during this golden time in their lives.

2. How to Make Them Comfortable

a) Regular Checkups

During this time in your Chiweenie's life, when their immune systems become weakened and they may be experiencing pain, you will want to get into the habit of taking your senior Chiweenie for regular veterinarian checkups.

Take them for a checkup every six months so that early detection of any problems can quickly be attended to and solutions for helping to keep your aging Chiweenie comfortable can be provided.

b) No Rough Play

An older Chiweenie will not have the same energy or willingness to play that they did when they were younger, therefore, do not allow younger children to rough house with an older dog. Explain to them that the dog is getting older and that as a result they must learn to be gentle and to leave the dog alone when it may want to rest or sleep.

c) Mild Exercise

Dogs still love going for walks, even when they are getting older and slowing down. Although an older Chiweenie will generally have less energy, they still need to exercise and keep moving, and taking them out regularly for shorter or slower walks will keep them healthier and happier long into old age.

d) Best Quality Food

Everyone has heard the saying, *"you are what you eat"* and for a senior dog, what he or she eats is even more important as his or her digestive system may no longer be functioning at peak performance.

Therefore, feeding a high quality, protein-based food will be important for a senior dog's continued health.

As well, if your older Chiweenie is overweight, you will want to help them shed excess pounds so that they will not be placing undue stress on their joints or heart.

The best way to accomplish this is by feeding smaller quantities of a higher quality food.

e) Clean and Parasite Free

The last thing an aging Chiweenie should have to deal with is the misery of itching and scratching, so make sure that you continue to give them regular baths with the appropriate shampoos and conditioners to keep their coat and skin comfortable and free from biting bugs.

f) Plenty of Water

Proper hydration is essential for helping to keep an older Chiweenie comfortable.

Water is life giving for every creature, so make certain that your aging dog has easy access to plenty of clean, fresh water which will help to improve their energy and digestion and also prevent dehydration which can add to joint stiffness.

g) Keep Them Warm

Just as older humans feel the cold more, so do older dogs.

Keeping your senior Chiweenie warm will help to alleviate some of the pain of their joint stiffness or arthritis. Make sure their bed or kennel is not kept in a drafty location and perhaps consider a heated bed for them.

Be aware that your aging Chiweenie will be more sensitive to extremes in temperature, and it will be up to you to make sure that they are comfortable at all times, which means not too hot and not too cold.

h) Indoor Clothing

We humans tend to wear warmer clothing as we get older, simply because we have more difficulty maintaining a comfortable body temperature and the same will be true of our senior Chiweenie companions.

Therefore, while you most likely already have a selection of outdoor clothing appropriate to the climate in which you live, you may not have considered keeping your Chiweenie warm while inside the home. Now would be the time to consider doggy t-shirts or sweater clothing options to help keep your aging companion comfortably warm both inside and out.

i) Steps or Stairs

If your Chiweenie is allowed to sleep on the human couch or chair, but they are having difficulties getting up there as their joints are becoming stiff and painful, consider buying or making them a set of soft, foam stairs so that they do not have to make the jump to their favorite sleeping place.

j) Comfortable Bed

While most dogs seem to be happy with sleeping on the floor, providing a padded, soft bed will greatly help to relieve sore spots and joint pain in older dogs.

If there is a draft in the home, generally it will be at floor level, therefore, a bed that is raised up off of the floor will be warmer for your senior Chiweenie.

k) More Love and Attention

Last, but not least, make sure that you give your senior Chiweenie lots of love and attention and never leave them alone for long periods of time.

When they are not feeling their best, they will want to be with you all that much more because you are their trusted guardian whom they love beyond life itself.

3. What is Euthanasia?

Every veterinarian will have received special training to help provide all incurably ill, injured or aged pets that have come to the end of their natural lives with a humane and gentle death, through a process called *"euthanasia"*.

When the time comes, euthanasia, or putting a dog *"to sleep"*, will usually be a two-step process.

First, the veterinarian will inject the dog with a sedative to make them sleepy, calm and comfortable.

Second, the veterinarian will inject a special drug that will peacefully stop their heart.

These drugs work in such a way that the dog will not experience any awareness whatsoever that their life is ending. What they will experience is very much like what we humans experience when falling asleep under anesthesia during a surgical procedure.

Once the second stage drug has been injected, the entire process takes about 10 to 20 seconds, at which time the veterinarian will then check to make certain that the dog's heart has stopped.

There is no suffering with this process, which is a very gentle and humane way to end a dog's suffering and allow them to peacefully pass on.

4. When to Help a Dog Transition

The impending loss of a beloved dog is one of the most painfully difficult and emotionally devastating experiences a canine guardian will ever have to face.

For the sake of our faithful companions, because we do not want to prolong their suffering, we humans will have to do our best to look at our dog's situation practically, rather than emotionally, so that we can make the best decision for them.

They may be suffering from extreme old age and the inability to even walk outside to relieve themselves, and thus having to deal with the indignity of regularly soiling their sleeping area, they may have been diagnosed with an incurable illness that is causing them much pain, or they may have been seriously injured.

Whatever the reason for a canine companion's suffering, it will be up to their human guardian to calmly guide the end-of-life experience so that any further discomfort and distress can be minimized.

a) What to Do If You Are Uncertain

In circumstances where it is not entirely clear how much a dog is suffering, it will be helpful to pay close attention to your Chiweenie's behavior and keep a daily log or record so that you can know for certain how much of their day is difficult and painful for them, and how much is not.

When you keep a daily log, it will be easier to decide if the dog's quality of life has become so poor that it makes better sense to offer them the gift of peacefully going to sleep.

During this time of uncertainty, it will also be very important to discuss with your veterinarian what signs of suffering may be associated with the dog's particular disease or condition, so that you know what to look for.

Often a dog may still continue to eat or drink despite being upset, having difficulty breathing, excessively panting, being disoriented or in much pain, and as their caring guardians, we will have to weigh their love of eating against how much they are really suffering in all other aspects of their life.

Obviously, if a canine guardian can clearly see that their beloved companion is suffering throughout their days and nights, it will make sense to help humanely end their suffering by planning a euthanasia procedure.

We humans are often tempted to delay the inevitable moment of euthanasia, because we love our dogs so much and cannot bear the anticipation of the intense grief we know will overwhelm us when we must say our final goodbyes to our beloved fur friend.

Unfortunately, we may regret that we allowed our dog to suffer too long, and could find ourselves wishing that if only we humans had the same option, to peacefully let go, when we find ourselves in such a stage in our own lives.

5. Grieving a Lost Pet

Some humans do not fully recognize the terrible grief involved in losing a beloved canine friend.

There will be many who do not understand the close bond we humans can have with our dogs, which is often unlike any we have with our human counterparts.

Your friends may give you pitying looks and try to cheer you up, but if they have never experienced such a loss themselves, they may also secretly think that you are making too much fuss over "just a dog".

For some of us humans, the loss of a beloved dog is so painful that we decide never to share our lives with another, because we cannot bear the thought of going through the pain of loss again.

Expect to feel terribly sad, tearful and yes, depressed because those who are close to their canine companions will feel their loss no less acutely than the loss of a human friend or life partner.

The grieving process can take some time to recover from, and some of us never totally recover.

After the loss of a family dog, first you need to take care of yourself by making certain that you keep eating and getting regular sleep, even though you will feel an almost eerie sense of loneliness.

Losing a beloved dog is a shock to the system, which can also affect your concentration and your ability to find joy or want to participate in other activities that may be part of your daily life.

During this early grieving time you will need to take extra care while driving or performing tasks that require your concentration as you may find yourself distracted.

If there are other dogs or pets in the home, they will also be grieving the loss of a companion, and may display this by acting depressed, being off their food or showing little interest in play or games. Therefore, you need to help guide your other pets through this grieving process by keeping them busy and interested, taking them for extra walks and spending more time with them.

Many people do not wait long enough before attempting to replace a lost pet and will immediately go to the local shelter and rescue a deserving dog.

While this may help to distract you from your grieving process, this is not really fair to the new fur member of your family.

Bringing a new pet into a home that is depressed and grieving the loss of a long time canine member may create behavioral problems for the new dog who will be faced with learning all about their new home while also dealing with the unstable, sad energy of the grieving family.

A better scenario would be to allow yourself the time to properly grieve by waiting a minimum of one month to allow yourself and your family to feel happier and more stable before deciding upon sharing your home with another dog.

The grieving process will be different for everyone and you will know when the time is right to consider sharing your home with another canine companion.

6. The Rainbow Bridge Poem

"Just this side of heaven is a place called Rainbow Bridge.

When an animal dies that has been
especially close to someone here,
that pet goes to Rainbow Bridge.
There are meadows and hills for all of our special friends
so they can run and play together.
There is plenty of food, water and sunshine,
and our friends are warm and comfortable.

All the animals who had been ill and old
are restored to health and vigor;
those who were hurt or maimed
are made whole and strong again,
just as we remember them in our dreams
of days and times gone by.
The animals are happy and content,
except for one small thing;

they each miss someone very special to them,
who had to be left behind.

They all run and play together,
but the day comes when one suddenly stops
and looks into the distance.
His bright eyes are intent; His eager body quivers.
Suddenly he begins to run from the group,
flying over the green grass,
his legs carrying him faster and faster.

You have been spotted,
and when you and your special friend finally meet,
you cling together in joyous reunion,
never to be parted again.
The happy kisses rain upon your face;
your hands again caress the beloved head,
 and you look once more into the trusting eyes
of your pet, so long gone from your life
but never absent from your heart.

Then you cross Rainbow Bridge together...."

- Author unknown

7. Memorials

There are as many ways to honor the passing of a beloved pet, as each of our fur friends is uniquely special to us.

For instance, you and your family may wish to have your companion cremated and preserve their ashes in a special urn or sprinkle their ashes along their favorite walk, or across the lake where they loved to swim.
Perhaps you will want to have a special marker, photo bereavement, photo engraved Rainbow Bridge Poem, or wooden plaque created in honor of your lost friend.

You may wish to keep their memory close to you at all times by having a DNA remembrance pendant or bracelet designed.

As well, there are support groups, such as Rainbow Bridge, which is a grief support community, to help you and your family through this painful period of loss and grief

Chapter 18: Rescue Organizations

When you are considering rescuing a specific breed of dog or puppy, the first place to start your search will be with your local breeders, shelters and rescue groups.

1. Shelters

Here you can expect to pay an adoption fee to cover the cost of spaying or neutering, but this will be only a small percentage of what you would pay a breeder, and you will be saving a life at the same time.

2. Online Resources

Sites such as Petango, Adopt A Pet and Pet Finder can be good places to begin your search.

Each of these online resources is a central gathering site for hundreds and hundreds of local shelters, humane societies and rescue groups.

3. Canine Clubs and Breeders

Another place to search will be hybrid clubs or breeders in your local area. These groups may have rescue dogs available.

Chapter 19: Resources & References

The following resources and references are listed alphabetically within their specific category and include web addresses.

1. Poison Control

ASPCA Poison Control [aspca.org]
Poisonous Plants Affecting Dogs - Cornell University, Department of Animal Science
[ansi.cornell.edu/plants/dogs/]

2. Breeders, Registries & Rescues

Adopt A Pet [adoptapet.com]
American Canine Hybrid Club [achclub.com]
Breeders Club [breedersclub.net/html/breeds/Chiweenie.htm]
California Designer Breeds Breeders
[http://designerbreeds.californiapuppiesforsale.com]
Designer Breed Registry [designerbreedregistry.com]
Designer Dogs Kennel Club [thekennelclub.org.uk]
Greenfield Puppies [greenfieldpuppies.com]
International Designer Canine Registry®
[designercanineregistry.com]
Little Rascals [littlerascalsuk.com]
National Dog Tattoo Register [dog-register.co.uk]
National Dog Registry [nationaldogregistry.com]
Petango [petango.com]
Pet Finder [petfinder.com]
Wentwood Poodogs [poodogs.co.uk]
Chiweenie's UK [Chiweeniesuk.com]

3. Equipment, Supplies & Services

Dog Bowl for Your Dog [dogbowlforyourdog.com]

Dremel™ Nail Grinder for Dogs
K-9 Super Heroes Dog Whispering
[k-9superheroesdogwhispering.com]
Modern Puppies [modernpuppies.com]
Poochie Bells™ [poochie-pets.net]
Remove Urine Odors [removeurineodors.com]
Sleepy Pod [sleepypod.com]
Tell Bell™ [tellbell.com]
ThunderShirt [thundershirt.com]

4. Memorials

Rainbow Bridge [rainbowbridge.com]

Published by IMB Publishing 2014

CPSIA information can be obtained
at www.ICGtesting.com
Printed in the USA
BVOW08s1125031217
501810BV00002B/299/P